GOD IS > GRIEF

HOW GOD'S GREATNESS TURNS DEATH INTO ETERNAL HOPE

Lisa Ann-Marie Stanford

God is > Than Grief
©2025 by Lisa Ann-Marie Stanford Brand

Published in the United States in assistance by Great Books.
ISBN 979-8-9939180-0-6

Scripture quotations are from the New King James (NKJV) version of the Bible. © Thomas Nelson, Inc. Publishers.

Scripture quotations taken from The Holy Bible, New International Version®, NIV®. Copyright © 1973, 1978, 1984, 2011 by Biblica, Inc. Used with permission of Zondervan. All rights reserved worldwide.

With the exception of brief quotations embodied in critical articles and reviews, no part of this book may be used, reproduced, or transmitted in any form or by any means, electronic or mechanical, including photocopying, recording, or by any information storage and retrieval system, without the prior written permission of the Publisher.

DEDICATION

To my father and my son. Thank you for our time together; it was shorter than I wanted it to be, but it was the most profound memory forever sketched in me. I love you.

FOREWORD

Losing a loved one evokes a range of emotions—grief, longing, and confusion. For us as believers, this journey can be both challenging and profound, deepening our understanding of God's promises about life after death. Reflecting on my own loss of my mother a year and a half ago, I have learned invaluable lessons about overcoming grief through God's grace.

For some Christians, and many unbelievers, death often carries a sense of finality, marking the conclusion of a life that may not have served its intended purpose. However, as believers, we are called to maintain a hopeful perspective on what lies ahead. One hundred percent of us will eventually transition out of this world, and how we spend our remaining time on Earth will ultimately determine how those left behind will handle our—or even their own—transition. This awareness prompts us to live with intention and purpose, touching lives in a Christlike manner.

During this time, the Word of God served as a profound source of comfort and strength as I have been battling and overcoming grief. The Scriptures have been a cherished source of comfort, and the Holy Spirit acts as our Comforter. When we invite Him into our hearts, grief loses its power to paralyze us or limit our movement in **God's** purpose and destiny for us. While grieving is a natural and necessary process, we must resist allowing it to dictate our outlook on life.

We must remember that Jesus is Lord of both the living and the dead. This crucial truth has provided me with great encouragement, and I hope it inspires you as well. As you read this book, I encourage you to dive deep into the Scriptures concerning the loss of a loved one, the nature of death, the promise of the afterlife, and how we ought to live our lives in light of these truths.

One of my favorite chapters, **1 Corinthians 15**, beautifully articulates our hope through the resurrected Jesus. This hope, dear brothers and sisters, should motivate us to hold fast to our faith, and not lose sight of the glorious outcome that awaits us. At the end of the day, we should recognize that we are engaged in the good fight of faith while remaining strong in the knowledge that our friends and loved ones who are in Christ and have since passed are with Him.

In a world where grief is prevalent, this book serves as a resource for those seeking healing. The author's journey through her own grief will guide you toward comfort and renewal. My prayer is that it profoundly impacts your life, leading you to discover His peace. Remember, Jesus is Lord of both the living and the dead—a truth that has encouraged me deeply.

FOREWORD

"Blessed are those who mourn, for they shall be comforted." (Matthew 5:4 ESV)

"He will wipe away every tear from their eyes, and death shall be no more, neither shall there be mourning, nor crying, nor pain anymore, for the former things have passed away." (Revelation 21:4 ESV)

By: Pastor Varney Taylor

PREFACE

This is…

A book proclaiming that God is greater than grief, I promise.

A memoir honoring my losses by turning pain into purpose.

A reminder of the inevitable and how to prepare.

A tool to receive healing in the midst of such a messy process I call grief.

He is the God among the living and the dead (*see Romans 14:9*), which means, above all else, He is God and He is indeed greater than.

TABLE OF CONTENTS

DEDICATION _____ iii

FOREWORD _____ v

PREFACE _____ ix

INTRODUCTION: THIS HITS HOME _____ xiii

PART I: BELOVED

CHAPTER 1: ZAIDEN-ROY _____ 3

CHAPTER 2: FINISHING HIS STORY _____ 15

CHAPTER 3: CROSSROADS:
WHERE PAIN & PURPOSE COLLIDE _____ 25

PART II: BEAUTY FOR ASHES

CHAPTER 4: THE WILDERNESS OF GRIEF _____ 47

CHAPTER 5: *WITH* GOD _____ 59

CHAPTER 6: JOB'S BLUEPRINT _____ 77

CHAPTER 7: THE END OF OLD,
THE BEGINNING OF NEW _____ 87

CHAPTER 8: LAMENTING WELL _____ 101

CHAPTER 9: YOUR NEW BEST FRIEND _____ 119

CHAPTER 10: THAT HEALETH THEE… _____ 131

PART III: BE READY

CHAPTER 11: THE GATES OF HEAVEN _____ 147

CHAPTER 12: TWO DESTINATIONS, ONE HOPE __ 161

EPILOGUE: MARY'S LOSS, GOD'S LOVE _____ 169

RECAP _____ 173

APPENDIX A _____ 175

ABOUT THE AUTHOR _____ 179

ACKNOWLEDGEMENTS _____ 181

INTRODUCTION:
THIS HITS HOME

"Some losses leave you paralyzed before they propel you forward."

In 2013, I lost my baby boy, Zaiden, at five months due to premature birth.

"He had a heartbeat" is what kept ringing in my head for months.

Ten days later, my father, Roy Stanford, died from metastatic pancreatic cancer.

"He was just progressing the other day" is what kept ringing in my head for months.

It's no secret that I questioned God many times over the past **twelve** years. This book may not be published yet, but here I am—writing about this journey over a decade later. **The number twelve represents divine order and government**, and I don't think it's a coincidence that in year twelve, I am finally able to speak about this from a healed perspective.

Being healed doesn't mean that I don't still grieve, cry, mourn, or feel the pain. Rather, being healed means I am whole and restored, and I have the comfort of the Lord to be a balm to my human pain. The truth is the comfort of the Lord was always available to me. But I didn't always seek or desire that comfort- that is the difference. The Word of God states that He sent His Word and healed them (**Psalm 107:20**), and that is something I can absolutely testify to once I invited Him into this process. I discovered that I did not have to do it all alone.

In this book, I want you to be encouraged. I want you to learn about grief—but more importantly, I want you to learn about God **right in** the midst of it all. Grief is messy, and it can feel like a storm. But after every storm, there is a rainbow, whether you see it or not. The promises of God still stand and in order for you to see it, you have to reposition yourself. You can either stand in front of grief or you can stand in front of God. Based on where your heart is positioned will determine what you choose to see and believe. Overall, I pray you leave this book with:

- a new hope
- a new heart
- a new way to pray and process as you deal with your own grief
- and a new grip on the promises God established thousands of years ago.

INTRODUCTION

To help you on this journey, I'd like to share my story with you, my father's story with you, and God's story for you—as you may be, or may know, someone who is dealing with grief and God at the same time. As you see on the front cover of this book, the leaf with a teardrop is used to alert people of a family or patient that endured a loss in the hospital so they get the quiet space they need. So, see this book as a moment to be quiet, to process, and to heal. At the beginning of each chapter, you'll find a quote of what I said or thought during my personal time of grief. Then at the end of each chapter, you'll find a section to land softly, with reflections, reminders, and key scriptures to read.

Remember, God is greater.

My Prayer for You

*Lord, I pray that whoever is reading this book is open and ready to hear from **You**. I pray **You** meet the needs of their heart and soothe every ounce of discomfort, grief, or pain. May they receive a fresh revelation of who **You** are in their lives, and may **You** be glorified throughout this entire book.*

*God, I ask **You** to comfort them and/or their loved ones and impart a divine restoration that can never be undone. Holy Spirit, give them the tools and guidance they need to move forward with **You**.*

*May the help they need certainly come from above. May this be the beginning of a fresh new start. Cause them to breathe without strain and trust in **You** without second-guessing.*

*Thank **You**, Jesus, that by Your stripes, we are healed and set free. **You** are the God who heals. **In Jesus Christ's name, Amen.***

PART I:
BELOVED

CHAPTER 1:
ZAIDEN-ROY

"But why did God have to take both?"

In 2012, I got pregnant around late September. To paint the full picture, at this time, I was a youth leader, mentor, and active participant at church. I really identified myself as an active churchgoer, but I truly desired more than just going to church. And even though my church **thoroughly** equipped me, I still struggled internally.

I started to seek out other vices to fill very deep voids. As a result, I ended up cheating on my then-boyfriend with someone else who I thought could fill that void. I was selfish.

I was desperate. And come to find out years later, I was hurting.

Once I found out I was pregnant, I began to question my walk with God even more. How could I, an active churchgoer, end up pregnant? Well, that's easy math when you are living in sin, but I was so naive at the time. I thought I was exempt, but I wasn't.

The pregnancy itself was a symptom of far larger and deeper issues I was very ignorant about and wanted to avoid. After deciding not to terminate my pregnancy, **honoring** my values as a believer, I chose to own my actions and take accountability.

I want to pause here and recognize the thoughts that I had about termination. I had to confront a lot of values I had as a believer, which honestly, is only qualified when you are in the situation. It is easy to judge others but until you are in such a position, you will be surprised at the thoughts, emotions, and things that will come up in your heart. This pregnancy revealed a lot of what was hidden and I had to face it all.

I went to church, **which was also** my place of employment, at the time, to confess and hold myself accountable to my youth pastor. I remember the tears in his eyes when I told him. As painful as it was to disappoint him, I had to be honest. After all, the house of God should be a place of solace and restoration.

When I finally told all my pastors and leaders what had happened, I was understandably asked to sit down from the ministries I served in. I received a mixture of reactions and emotions, including judgment, shame, guilt, empathy, sadness, disappointment, and most importantly, love.

I remember being held far more accountable than my baby's father, which hurt me even more. I had a lot to lose, and I lost it. I lost the titles, status, and respect as a leader to many young people. My life literally felt like it was falling apart because I had built my life based on what people thought of me at a very young age.

Now, to be clear, I stand by and appreciate what my church leaders and pastors did. Back then, I didn't fully understand, but now, as an adult, I truly understand and approve of **loving correction** in the church. When you break an arm, you can't continue to use it as before. You put it in a cast to heal and rehabilitate the broken pieces. Godly discipline and correction (not punishment) should bring restoration, discipleship, and ultimately spiritual growth. My pastors had no authority over how others handled the situation, so this is not a church-bashing moment. This reflects my human experience, and though it was my first experience with church hurt, I recognize in some ways how it was what was best for me at the time.

"To whom much is given, much is required."
(Luke 12:48)

And I dropped the ball on that. A few years prior, my father was diagnosed with stage 3 pancreatic cancer and was receiving aggressive treatment. Not only did we have to prepare for a baby, but we also had to continue to care for my father.

I vividly remember the day I looked into my dad's eyes and noticed how yellow they were. That prompted him to go to the doctor immediately. Who knew I would be facing two diagnoses two years apart, one that evoked life and one that evoked the fear of death.

We battled through a range of emotions as a family, but by the time everyone came to terms with my pregnancy, we were actually happy to welcome this baby boy. I remember hearing his heartbeat and feeling his flutters early in the morning. I started to embrace the fact that I was about to be a boy mom **before being a boy mom was a trend.**

Looking back, I think this baby gave me hope. He gave me a reason to live. With everything my family was going through with my dad's illness, I needed something bigger than myself to keep going.

My father was a covering for me. So, to see him so broken and fragile left me broken and fragile too. But this baby positioned me to become a covering myself, and I didn't take that lightly.

Fast forward to **January 2013:** Things with my father started to decline rapidly. His cancer had spread to his liver, and though it had been shrinking months before, it was now spreading again. Chemotherapy and radiation were weakening him. He continued working full-time during this time, but it reached a point where he had to stop.

My father had months' worth of PTO he never used. He loved to work, and he was good at it.

How can such an active man become like a little boy again? I wondered.

It was crippling to see him lose himself. I felt helpless. But I could only imagine how he felt trapped in a body that seemingly betrayed him. Soon and very soon, I would feel the same way about mine.

By the end of January, my father was admitted to Johns Hopkins Hospital, and I started experiencing a lot of pressure and contractions at the same time. I went to the doctor's office, where they provided me with fluids because I was dehydrated.

I didn't understand how that was possible with all the water I had been drinking—but that's neither here nor there.

After I became stable, they sent me home. Not knowing what I know now, I should have gone straight to the hospital to be admitted, since my cervix was already dilating.

By evening, I was in pain again, but even worse, I started having contractions so intense that I stripped everything off, hoping that would help. Nothing did.

I remember going to the bathroom and feeling something come out—my mucus plug. I yelled for my mother, who called the ambulance as I laid on the bathroom floor in agony. They came quickly and took me to the nearest hospital.

As I was triaged, I learned I was in preterm labor. My baby had an active heartbeat, but nothing in the world could stop the labor, or so they said. My baby boy was still fighting for his life, but my body was fighting against me. *At least, that's how I processed it at the time.*

I remember the nurse holding my hand and saying, *"It will be alright."* They started the pain medication and waited until I was ready to push. I remember the urges, still hearing his heartbeat, and not fully grasping what was going to happen. By the third urge, I was ready to push. My sister and mother helped me push as I felt the pressure of my baby boy being born.

At 20 weeks, he was not able to breathe on his own. And unfortunately, the hospital didn't have an acute-level NICU to resuscitate him.

So, there he was, in my arms, twitching and moving, until there was no more life left in him.

This was the moment I felt like my body betrayed me. This was the moment I met life and death at the same time. This was the moment I filled out a birth and death certificate on 2/1/13. This was the moment I related to my father in the deepest way.

Who knew this would be our most vulnerable moment?

At the time, I didn't realize it, but God was beginning to untangle some of the lies I had believed about myself, my body, and His love. I didn't see the healing yet. I didn't feel hope. But something was shifting, even as I stepped into the next valley — my father's death.

I was discharged the next day, and my father was still admitted at Johns Hopkins Hospital. I could hear how disappointed he was when he heard the news because Zaiden-Roy was supposed to be his representative **when** he left this earth. That was our little promise and the way we decided to cope with losing each other. We both figured Zaiden-Roy would be the piece that kept us close. After all, Zaiden was so long, so I knew he would be tall like my dad. And he had my nose, which I got from my dad too. He was supposed to be the healing agent. But **that was** just not how the story ended.

Not **long** after I was discharged, I was back to school, finishing up my last semester of college. I was visiting my father at the hospital and quickly pivoted to helping my mother again. Life kept going. Life did not wait for me to mourn my loss. Life does not wait for anyone.

Similar to what the nurse told me, the doctors told my father there was nothing else **they could do.** He was admitted into hospice care and **prepared** to come home. In preparation for him to come home, a hospital social worker came to meet with us. It **was at this moment** I learned about medical social work and a specialization in maternal-child health. I remember my father immediately telling me, *"Lisa, I want you to work here"*—at Johns Hopkins Hospital, that is—and I **clung tightly to** that desire of his. But in the moment, I put a pin in that and continued to focus on my father.

He was discharged home on 2/9/13 and as the ambulance dropped him off, I remember him saying, *"I am ready to go home"* as he climbed the stairs to his room. We all knew which "home" he was referring to. We knew what was coming, and the weeks the doctors predicted **turned out to be** two days. During these two days, we rallied around him as much as we could. My siblings were planning to visit **him from New Jersey/New York**, and we called out to elders/pastors to come pray, but it was too late.

I remember I was at my internship on 2/11/13, the day his jaw became locked and he was unable to talk much. My father was a strong man and didn't want morphine, so I could only imagine the pain he was in. The nurse advised that he was fine, but the Holy Spirit prompted me to leave and hurry back home.

I had my best friends with me and saw my dad looking **different from** when I saw him that morning. He tried to engage but couldn't. He asked to watch *Family Feud* one more time, and we laid there and watched it. He loved Steve Harvey's suits and this was our favorite show to watch together.

I then decided to leave and get a bite to eat, holding back my tears, and I uttered, *"Daddy, I love you, but hold on, please."* because I knew my siblings were coming the next day. He uttered, *"I love you too,"* muffled by his trapped airway. I could tell he was fighting even on his last breath. He did not want to go. He was holding on.

I went down the street and came back by the time my mother was home from work. She asked me to take the nurse to the train station, which I did. Once I got back, she said, *"Go check on your father. He is breathing heavily."* I went up the stairs and suddenly felt this daunting feeling. I knew — I just knew.

I yelled out, *"Daddy,"* how I usually would. No response. I yelled it again, a little stronger this time — still no response. And there he was, on the other side of the bed, passed away to the other side **into eternity**. I grabbed him and screamed. I said, *"Noooooo, don't go."* It was just odd, to be honest. I knew it was his time, yet I also did not know it was his time.

There was a dialectical experience — between peace and sadness at the same time. This was my very first experience of two opposing things being true at once. Here I was at the end of my father's life, and the beginning of a whole new path for me.

My mother came up and we called hospice and the ambulance, who took his body from our home. I can't even begin to describe how I felt at that moment. On one hand, I felt grateful that God prompted me to come home when I did, so I could say *I love you* one last time, because otherwise, I would have missed that moment. On the other **hand**, I felt like a failure because I couldn't save him.

I have no clue what it would have been like to see him actively transition, but I know God was with him. The Word says, *"To be absent from the body is to be present with the Lord"* (2 Corinthians 5:8). But regardless of the number of scriptures I knew, I was going through a turmoil of real human emotions. This was not a time to quote scripture; This was a time to lean on it — and I didn't know how to do that nor did I want to.

This was a turning point in my life, my faith, and my identity. But before I found myself again by God's grace, I went through **a wilderness** of ups and downs.

It was as if my son being *"taken"* wasn't enough. Every truth in me turned into lies. I could not believe God did this to me. My pain became the excuse I used to forget God.

Instead of allowing Him in to heal me, I believed that He was out to hurt me — which is clearly a lie from hell. But at that moment, that's all I knew. And the lies, the pain, the void, the grief became much more comforting than the truth. This is where I chose to stand and as I mentioned in the introduction, based on where you stand will determine what you choose to see and believe.

February 1st, I lost my baby boy, my little glimpse of hope and ten days later, February 11th, I lost my father, my covering, my hero. February 2013 was the mark of losing a huge piece of me.

Though I did not know how or when, eventually God worked this into His ultimate plan for my life, as it says in Romans 8:28, *"And we know that in all things God works for the good of those who love him, who have been called according to his purpose."*

Stay tuned for that. The journey continues.

DEVOTIONAL REFLECTION

READ:

Isaiah 61:3 – "To all who mourn in Israel, he will give a crown of beauty for ashes, a joyous blessing instead of mourning, festive praise instead of despair. In their righteousness, they will be like great oaks that the LORD has planted for his own glory."

REFLECT:

Take some time to reflect on this chapter. How has losing your loved one impacted your relationship with God?

REMEMBER:

"Though I did not know how or when, eventually God worked this into His ultimate plan for my life"… He will do the same for you.

CHAPTER 2:
FINISHING HIS STORY

"I'll always be your twin."

For the longest time I was a daddy's girl. I look exactly like him and even now, I recognize a lot of the same mannerisms he had in myself. This book would not be complete without what he started. I would like to share the manuscript he started writing before he passed away. I remember how badly he wanted the world to know that God healed him—hence the name of his book, "You Can Be Healed and Be Blessed." As a way to honor him, I wanted to include his side of the story using his own words. Though the story didn't end the way we hoped, his story still carries strength and could hopefully help someone on their own journey through grief. Though this story isn't complete, I hope you are still able to find some encouragement.

Daddy, I hope this makes you smile. It's an honor to continue your story.

YOU CAN BE HEALED AND BE BLESSED

By: Roy G. Stanford

Chapter 1: Just Believe

My name is Roy Stanford, and I would like to share my story of believing in God, trusting in Him and His will, **which made** the impossible become possible.

*Ever since an early age, about seven, I was baptized in the Catholic Church, having been brought up in a Christian family. I was **committed to living a godly life. I didn't swear or curse and attended church every Sunday.***

My first experience with God's power of blessing came at about the age of 21. I was supporting a family of two and making five English pounds per week. I had a young wife and one child and was also taking care of my parents. Life was a struggle at 21 years of age.

Every night, I would pray to God to give me another job, just to make seven pounds fifty, or 50% more pay. I prayed earnestly every night.

And then, it happened.

I replied to an ad for an electrical technician job. I was in night school studying to be an electrical engineer but had to give that up because of financial difficulties. So this job was needed. It was about seventy miles away from home, in the country. Seventy miles in Jamaica is a long way; it takes about two hours going over the mountain. I had never gone more than ten miles from Kingston.

On the morning of the interview, which was at 10:00 a.m., I took a taxi to the country for the first time and at the same time, the devil started his plan.

First, I arrived for the interview late. I tried to explain to the interviewer that I was from a faraway city and the taxi made me late. He said, "I'm sorry, but I can't give you the test."

I walked away crying. I only had enough money to get back home, so I had no lunch. I had to return to face my friends and family, who thought I was hopeless and wouldn't amount to anything.

I said a prayer right away: "My God, what have I done?"

Immediately, the interviewer came running after me and said, "Come take the test." I took the test and finished first in the class.

God's Holy Spirit was working in the interviewer, even though the interviewer had no idea he was being used in such a way.

That's how God works. He uses whatever and whoever He wants to supply all our needs. I know it's because I had been praying every day for a better job and trusting in God. As a result, I received what I asked for — plus more. Instead of 50% more, God gave me 300% more.

So whatever you ask God to do in your life, expect Him to do it above and beyond. All through prayer and simply believing, He completely blessed me with the job. I became the youngest foreman, then the youngest supervisor, and also the youngest superintendent.

Naturally, I couldn't have received this job. It was supernatural. Everything I prayed for was manifested through Christ Jesus.

So pray constantly for whatever it is you need, for all your desires, and God will grant you more than you could ever imagine. Just believe!

Chapter 2: Humility Opens Doors

After a few years on the job, I stopped going to church and started indulging in drinking, among other things. I was following my friends, and guess what happened?

*It left open doors in my life that allowed the enemy to come in and blind me from my blessings, **especially later in my career**. As a result, life became a burden, and my marital life was falling apart.*

My first wife migrated to the United States, and I eventually left and came to the U.S. with two of my eldest children. I had an interview for a job at the transit company and was told the job was mine, but they needed more proof of my qualifications.

I provided what they asked for, but they still put me on hold. It was a hard thing to wake up to, caring for three grown kids with no job.

The lady I was renting a small bedroom from, along with my two boys, suggested that I go to her church and pray.

So I went to church on a Sunday morning, and I prayed all day.

That night, the Lord spoke to me and said, "Roy, be humble and tell the lady that you will take a car cleaning job."

The next day, I called her and said I was willing to take a car cleaning job until an electrical job became available. I called the following morning, and sure enough, I got the job.

This was another blessing from God and a lesson in humility. He needed me to humble myself so He could bless me.

I am still working for the transit company and have been for the past twenty-five years, with God's blessing.

Remember to trust Him. Pray for all your desires. Humble yourself and if it aligns with His will, He will grant it to you.

And this is where his manuscript ended. Though short, I learned a lot about my dad as I read this. I remember him asking me to edit it—and just weeks later, the cancer got worse.

My biggest takeaways from this are faith, humility, and unmerited favor. It's interesting because **those traits described my dad** during his course of treatment. My father still worked during treatment; he prayed every day about his sickness, and we found favor with his treatment, surgeon, and even in the years of life we were granted.

Those who know about pancreatic cancer know it is an aggressive cancer — one that is hard to detect until about stage 3 or 4, with little time to live. Even with its standard poor prognosis, my father lived **a year and a half** longer than the doctors expected. That was God's mercy.

We found one of the best doctors at Johns Hopkins Hospital, who performed a **nine-hour** surgery to preserve his life. That was God's favor.

I could imagine my father telling more of his story — his feelings about his illness and how God's healing during his lifetime changed his life. It wasn't the healing of his physical illness, but rather that God saved his soul. During his years of battling cancer, he fully converted to Christianity, began attending church with my mother and me (after years of going separately), and was baptized. His send-off was beautiful, and I am blessed to share how **God's healing of him has changed me**. Maybe my dad didn't heal the way we wanted him to, but he is healed on the other side of eternity.

Let this be a reminder and word of encouragement for you:

Believe in God. Trust Him.
Pray earnestly. Stay humble.

It's humbling for me to know even a little bit about my father's upbringing, because can you imagine how hard it was to access opportunity back then? Life was hard for him and my mother — and I appreciate their sacrifices.

The beginning of this book shows great trust and strength in God, no matter how much you lose your way through the ups and downs of life. You never know how life will twist and turn, but in the end, God has the final say. Whether that be on this side of earth or on that side of heaven, we must hold on to Him as **the Author and Finisher of our faith** (see Hebrews 12:2). We must also know that God is present with us when we are absent from our bodies, for it says:

> *"We are confident, yes, well pleased rather to be absent from the body and to be present with the Lord."* (2 Corinthians 5:8)

After reading my father's story, I hope you find hope. God is no respecter of persons, so the same way He showed up supernaturally for us, I believe He can do the same for you. The same way we found favor in his process, I believe favor can be found for you too.

In the end, God still kept His promise — to be faithful, to be present, and to be merciful. It may not have been my preferred version of healing, but after years of struggling with grief, I see it differently now. And I pray that by the end of this book, you see it differently too.

And so — this piece of work from my dad is to give God that glory.

DEVOTIONAL REFLECTION

READ:

Psalm 5:12—*"Surely, LORD, you bless the righteous; you surround them with your favor as with a shield."*

REFLECT:

Take some time to reflect on these chapters. How has God's favor, mercy, and grace showed up during this time of grief for you?

REMEMBER:

"Remember to trust Him. Pray for all your desires. Humble yourself—and if it aligns with His will, He will grant it to you."

CHAPTER 3:
CROSSROADS: WHERE PAIN & PURPOSE COLLIDE

"The same place that hurt me is the same place that God used to heal me."

One of the beautiful things God does is make all things work together for the good of those who love Him and are called according to His purpose (see Romans 8:28). Whenever I reflect on this scripture, I imagine the back of a tapestry crochet. The weaving takes time and as each thread is pulled through, it looks like a clump of mess at the back with no direction or sense of clarity.

But when it is finished, all you see is the beautiful masterpiece on the front and that is what people remember- the finished product. However, during the weaving journey, the process of working all things together, it is not as beautiful as the finished product looks.

Pain and purpose are two completely different concepts, yet only God in all His wisdom and sovereignty can masterfully work it all together for our good. That is a promise. But the caveat here that most people skip over is this promise is for those who love Him and are called according to His purpose.

There are some paths you can take that may not turn out as beautiful. Why? Because we have free will and if our will decides to believe what pain, the enemy, and our grief is telling us, then that is what will dictate what is to come. But if you surrender, yield, and allow God to love you back to your purpose, He will use every single thread to make it work out for *your* good.

On average, it takes weeks, months, and even years to weave a tapestry depending on the size, intricacy of colors and patterns, the weaver's skill level, and complexity. So just imagine God weaving every experience, circumstance, grief, setback, success, and background with our already complex human nature. It takes years! But what I love about God is He is the most patient lover.

No matter how many threads you created in this tapestry to create your own design, as you yield to Him, He makes it work. What a creative God we serve. He is more dedicated to the process of restoration, transformation, and healing than we are. That is why **Ecclesiastes 3:11** says:

> *He has made everything beautiful in its time. He has also set eternity in the human heart; yet no one can fathom what God has done from beginning to end.*

No one can predict how God will make it work, especially when life's surprises come our way like losing a loved one suddenly or losing a loved one who died a slow death. It is beyond our limitations; therefore, no one can fathom what God will do from beginning to end. He is the best potter, carpenter, and weaver there is and in the end it is beautiful.

So, as you read this chapter, I am going to share my personal crossroads. I came to this point many times and sometimes I chose pain and finally, I chose purpose. As you read it, it may seem a little all over the place and that is intentional. It was messy just like the back of that tapestry, so just imagine going through that rollercoaster process. It was hard, but in the end, God worked it out for my good.

I hope you have your tea or coffee in hand.

May 2013

Shortly after the passing of my father and baby boy, I graduated from undergrad college and decided to take a year off to work full-time and apply to graduate school. During this time, I struggled with depression, low self-esteem, and residual trauma. I used many vices to cope because I was too angry with God. I barely trusted people and found myself unhealthy, and **I wasn't** really confronting the pain I was experiencing.

I engaged in minimal therapy at the time, which was helpful, but to be honest, I didn't have the willingness to deal with my trauma or depression. I was just too tired. I would pray and still participate in ministry, go to church, but I was just going through the motions. It was a conflicting time of my life because the same place that hurt me is the same place I found refuge and safety.

I remember hearing a scripture one day, which has stuck with me ever since. It is Isaiah 40:31:

> *"But those who wait on the Lord shall renew their strength, they shall mount up with wings like eagles, they shall run and not be weary, they shall walk and not faint."*

And another translation says *"but those who hope in the Lord…"* I didn't fully grasp the meaning of it, but it hit me like a ton of bricks. I felt weary. I felt like fainting. I felt like giving up. Yet this scripture immediately brought me solace, comfort, and hope. This is why each chapter ends with a pillar of hope, the Word of God.

Even though I was not interested in fully re-establishing my relationship with God, He was always interested in me. Little did I know He gave me a Word that would follow me throughout every season to come.

The first year of grief is the toughest. Everything reminded me of my father and my son and there was nothing that could make me feel better, so I thought. Life kept going so I had no choice but to keep going. It felt quite disrespectful if I am being honest. I wish there was a guideline on what to do next after losing a loved one, but sadly there wasn't.

During this time, I was trying to figure out my life without my father. I had to confront my anticipated due date without a baby. I had postpartum symptoms without a baby which no one really talks about. I had to confront leaders, friends, and family members who looked at me with shame, pity, and sympathy at the same time.

I had a lot of support yet I still felt alone. Losing a parent is like losing a covering. I was naked and I realized how vulnerable and uncomfortable it was as I began to celebrate milestones, holidays, and life events without them. The days leading up to their one year anniversary were heavy and nothing can truly prepare you for it.

You have no idea what to expect or how you'll feel. It is a very unpredictable space and everyone is just watching you grieve without knowing the right words to say. It can tear up families or bring families closer. It is lonely and the silence is deafening.

After about 3 months of the person being gone, the calls stop, the check-ins decrease, and you are figuring it out every single day. You really do not realize how much space a person takes up in your life until they are gone.

February 2014

Shortly after my father and son's first year death anniversary, I started sharing my feelings and process on social media- back then social media was my outlet. Imagine a vinyl record machine playing the same song over and over as it spins. That is what the first year anniversary felt like.

I remembered every single detail and it was suffocating so I found a way to express myself online. Looking back, it must've been a mess because how I write about it now is not how I was writing about it then. I was openly going through a raw process, but let's remember the tapestry analogy.

I wanted to share my story not really knowing where it would go. I was beginning to realize that not only had I lost two people physically, I had also lost myself emotionally. I lost a sense of identity, my culture, and who I was as a person. I had no clue how I was going to get that back.

In Fall 2014, I started graduate school. I moved out of my family's home, only about an hour away to Baltimore. It may sound silly to move out when I didn't need to, but I also needed that time away. I needed space to grow up and also give space for my family to grieve.

They were all grieving my dad, but I was grieving two people—two incidents, back to back—and I needed to honor that alone. It appeared selfish to many, but I was desperate for some kind of fresh air. The only way out at the time was to physically move.

I started to enjoy being on my own and engaging in school. It was a good distraction. I started to "do me" which felt liberating because my mama was strict which my future self now appreciates. That's the Caribbean blood. I started drinking, partying, dating multiple people, and becoming less sensitive to and less interested in the things of God.

To put it frankly, I backslid. And my purpose slipped further and further away. Because of me living so far away from family, friends, or church, I numbed myself. I tried to keep up with the ministry but eventually that dissipated.

I thought I was healing, but I was really just covering up a wound, which came back up years later. I was weaving in some really bad choices during this time and honestly didn't care about the cost.

May 2016

Even though I was going through all of that emotionally and spiritually over the last two years, I was succeeding in school. I was able to specialize in Maternal-Child Health which allowed me to intern at a community program called B'more for Healthy Babies and at University of Maryland Medical Center on Labor & Delivery. Coincidence I think not.

Right before I graduated, I started to apply to jobs. Unfortunately, my internship didn't have any open slots. Upon looking, I saw a vacancy at Johns Hopkins Hospital. I initially applied to be a general pediatric social worker just to get in the door. But when the director met with me, she told me they just opened up one vacant position in Postpartum/Labor & Delivery. Due to my prior school internships, she offered me the job on the spot.

In May 2016, I graduated with a job offer at Johns Hopkins Hospital, the same place my dad once told me he wanted me to work– a purposefully weaving moment from God I was not worthy of.

Though I was going through so much personal pain and had become faithless to the things of God, yet and still, He remained faithful and answered the desires of my heart—and the desires of my late father's heart too.

I started working shortly after graduating and moving out into my own apartment since I was initially living in my school's housing. I found so much fulfillment working with moms. I don't even call them patients, I call them moms because as soon as that baby is delivered, whether deceased or alive, you step right into your motherhood role. I met with women from all over the world, given the complex cases seen at Johns Hopkins Hospital. These women needed hope too. These were:

- Moms who had to stay in the hospital for safety precautions.
- Moms who experienced loss, even at full term.
- Moms who had been assaulted by their partners.
- Moms with severe mental illness.
- Moms who didn't know how to bond with their babies.
- Moms recovering from C-sections who still found the strength to visit their babies in the NICU.
- Moms who were addicted to substances and while wrestling with their babies withdrawing, used this as an opportunity to get into treatment.
- Moms who were teenagers and needed to know their life still had purpose.
- Moms who were surrounded by good support systems—and others who weren't.
- Moms who needed an advocate.

- Moms who made the difficult decision to give their child up for adoption.
- Moms who simply needed someone to hold their hand in their most vulnerable moment.

It was at this time of my life where I realized that my pain wasn't pointless. It was the beginning of a deeper purpose. There God goes weaving again.

They thought I was their social worker, helping them adjust to their baby, or lack thereof, but really, I was their patient.

- There were times I felt triggered.
- There were times I was reminded of my pain.
- There were times I cried along with them.
- There were times I was hopeful.

This was a time of my life that began the journey of restoration. Unbeknownst to this job, God used it to start healing me and birth a new purpose. The flashbacks of me pushing out a baby who would die was now being replaced with serving so many women during one of most beautiful, yet scary and vulnerable moments.

> *"The same place that hurt me is the same place that God used to heal me."*

Not to mention, I learned so much as a social worker there, and those skills and friendships I made along the way are still with me.

October 2018

I'm grateful that God brought me to a full-circle moment and allowed me to see His hand turning something awful into something good (remember Romans 8:28). At that point, I decided to do more with what I'd been given.

Around this time, I felt the urge to start a women's empowerment company based off of a scripture that touched me deeply during my earlier years of grief– Proverbs 31:10. It says, *"she is worth far more than rubies."* With this scripture, I was beginning to re-identify my own worth—the worth I thought I lost back in 2013.

It was time to get back to God, to get back to my purpose and calling, and to get back to who I was called to be. Truth be told, going back wasn't going to be easy, but I was willing to walk the path.

This was my crossroads— I made the choice to allow God to make my pain into purpose seeing that He was already weaving towards that pattern anyways.

To officially launch my organization, I wrote a blog about my journey, held women's empowerment events, and started posting more relatable content on social media about my healing. The spiraling had slowed down at this point.

I was still trying to figure things out along the way. I got re-engaged at my church, continued rebuilding with my family, and was surrounded by great friends. I ended an unhealthy relationship and promised God to do it His way, I started my fitness journey and overall, things seemed to look positive on the outside.

One of the things that brought me joy during my years of grief, despair and loneliness were affirmations. I used affirmations as a way to solve my self-worth and self-esteem issues. Instead of relying on others to affirm me as heavily as I did, I needed to invest that into myself.

I started randomly posting affirmations, and eventually, it developed into my first book called My Words of Affirmation, where I shared my story, my affirmations, and God's Word. I remember writing my first draft of this book in the hospital setting back in 2018 and it was later published in 2020.

The gap between writing it and publishing it illustrates what was happening to me internally. Like I mentioned, outwardly things seemed positive, because I did a really good job at looking perfect, but inwardly I still struggled with my faith, relationships, family issues, financial burdens, and tumultuous emotions– Another thread is going in right here.

March 2020

Then COVID happened. As we all know, many of us had to come to terms with a lot of things we left hidden in the closet or under the rug, as we were all forced to be at home with ourselves. It was in this very same year I began a new relationship, started finishing my first book, and was getting ready to turn the infamous 30 years old.

Finally publishing the book opened the door to me consistently affirming myself. It sort of became its own thing that I started to consistently share on social media. The same relationship I started this year also ended this year, right after publishing that book — and it stung.

I started to realize a pattern. Every time something discouraging or disappointing would occur, I felt like I was going back to that girl in 2013. I would feel all the pain from over the years as if it just occurred. I would revert back to the self-hatred, God-blaming, shame, pity, and dysregulation. What a mess of threads.

At this point, noticing this cycle, I had two choices; I could go down the path of self-sabotage and destruction as I usually did, or I could do something different to get a different result.

January 2021

By this time, it was 2021 and I decided to yield completely to God in a new, fresh way.

I mean, geez, by this time, I had already rededicated my life to God about three times (lol). As I said earlier, I came to this crossroads many times and the weaving of this tapestry had a little bit of self-infliction but with a lot of God's grace through every picking. Picking is the process of passing the weft thread, which creates the design.

Something about this time felt different though.

I told God, *"This is it. Unless You speak to me directly, I'm going to just live a life in sin and let go of the little glimpses of hope and purpose You gave me."*

I needed a personal encounter with Him and I was bold with that request.

A few months into the year, after I purchased and moved into my first owned home, I had that personal encounter.

God brought someone into my life who spoke directly to me — and the things they said could only have been known by God — He is skillful with weaving isn't He.

This was God's merciful weaving. Because, to be honest, God didn't owe me anything. He chooses to reveal Himself to His people, so I knew the prayer I prayed was dangerous. But for God to take the time to send someone to speak to me — that was the greatest love letter I ever received.

From that moment, I said a final yes, and I've never turned back.

May 2021- January 2023

To help me with rededicating my life, I had a Christian life coach. I started reading more faith-based personal development books and listening to more sermons, in addition to attending my home church more regularly. I returned to ministry after years of not being actively involved. Me and my family grew closer and I started investing in how to take care of myself in a healthier manner.

During these years, purpose-related content kept tugging at my heart. I wanted to have a stronger presence on social media, but I wasn't sure how. Remember, I used this same space as an outlet for pain, so I was dedicated to using it for purpose.

I tried doing what other people were doing, but it didn't click. Then I was reminded by the Holy Spirit to continue affirming people—but this time, He told me to start with myself again.

At that point, I wasn't really reading the Word of God in a disciplined way. So God told me to start reading His Word consistently—and to affirm myself from there.

Like a baby, I started in Genesis—and I'm still working my way through. As He leads, I read. But overtime I noticed, His Word started to become food for me- another thread.

For months, I would write down scriptures and place them on my mirror, repeating them daily. Beforehand, I would just write down affirmations. Things like:

I am beautiful. I am smart. I am going to make it.

Those are cool, but now I needed affirmations that held weight and power.

I needed to be affirmed in His Word and His truths. And once I did that, I had the biggest epiphany.

AH-HA! This was the missing ingredient the whole time: HIS WORD! (lightbulb moment)

As I started to read His Word, affirm myself in His truths, transformation was taking place on the inside of me. Restoration actually became possible.

After doing this for some time, I felt peace about sharing it on social media—which has now become its own thing.

In 2021, God led me to start Morning Word & Affirmations, where the Word of God is our declaration and the affirmations are based on His Word. The very same year God confronted me after my bold prayer.

I was so scared initially, because I knew this wouldn't be a super popular thing initially. I also knew I would need to keep doing the work behind the scenes — which I had failed to do before.

But thank God for His grace enabling me to do it. Thank God He renewed my strength over and over again — so that I've been able to do this for 3+ years straight.

To God be the glory! I feel like this is where the tapestry design started to form.

The words I started writing have grown over the years. I am now more bold with my affirmations. What we loose in heaven shall be loosed on earth, and affirming His truths is imperative. It's spiritual warfare, honestly.

Now, it is at the point where I have decided to make it its own platform: Affirmed & True — where people are planted in His law and Word so that it can produce good fruit in its season (Psalm 1:3). The page has over 20k followers and though I am currently rebranding it into something bigger out of obedience to God, it is still standing.

Through the three years I started this platform, it wasn't about the platform at all. God was literally nursing me back to health, The Holy Spirit started to reveal the rotten old pieces of pain that were lingering every year which is why I kept repeating a cycle, Jesus became more real to me than ever and through His grace, I overcame so much more that was hidden behind the mask of grief.

Years 2024-2025

After all this time, we are now 12 years later, and without me even sharing every single detail I am sure you can hear how much of a messy journey it has been. But by the grace of God, I am more healed than ever.

    I turned the women's empowerment organization into my private practice, Worth Above Rubies Christian Counseling. I am rebranding Affirmed & True.

    I am spending so much quality time with my family, making memories that will last for years to come, as we are all in a much healthier place. I am actively involved at my church, mentoring young girls and emerging as a core leader.

    I am surrounded by mentors, friends, and a village that weathered the storms with me. I take care of myself by loving being alone instead of needing a man to fill a void. I dedicated myself to years of therapy and work with the fellowship of the Holy Spirit.

    I am free from pain, shame, and worthlessness. I am free from the opinions of others and even the narrative of my grief. I have moments as a human being, but I am not blaming God when His plan to heal my dad on the other side now brings peace.

    I am no longer ashamed of my body and I await my gifts in the shape of a beautiful family. His comfort has held my tears. I am no longer a slave to sin or the idol of being a victim. I am a victor.

    This verse resonates here:

> *"But by the grace of God I am what I am, and his grace to me was not without effect. No, I worked harder than all of them – yet not I, but the grace of God that was with me."* (1 Corinthians 15:10)

God worked it ALL together. God used my grief to transform me. He didn't miss a piece of thread or detail and He never does. The work God has done for me is a testament of His love, as He will always search for His sheep.

> *No power in the sky above or in the earth below – indeed, nothing in all creation will ever be able to separate us from the love of God that is revealed in Christ Jesus our Lord."* (Romans 8:39)

The Journey Continues

I am launching this book towards the end of 2025 into early 2026. What a journey and because we never "arrive", the journey continues.

There was so much to take away from this chapter as crazy of a ride it was. Here are the major takeaways I want you to remember:

- The most effective weapon, tool, or source of help that made this turning point possible was The Word of God.

> *"For the word of God is alive and active. Sharper than any double-edged sword, it penetrates even to dividing*

soul and spirit, joints and marrow; it judges the thoughts and attitudes of the heart." Hebrews 4:12

- The process takes time; it will not be a quick fix, easy, comfortable, or clear.
- Even when we stray from God's divine plan, He is still faithful to us.
- He hears the desires of our heart when we can't speak.
- Someone had to be praying for me cause whew. You need prayerful people in your life.
- There are practical things He wants you to do just as much as there are spiritual things you need to do. He uses both — and we'll lay these out in another chapter.
- Grief can become a mask and if you are not careful, it will hide dormant issues that have nothing to do with it.
- Double for your trouble is real.
- It isn't always about you, sad to say, there is something greater.
- You must willingly choose, participate, yield, and surrender. That is a pre-requisite for the process.

Lastly and most importantly, thanks for reading my journey. I'm sure the tea or coffee is done.

DEVOTIONAL REFLECTION

READ:

Romans 8:28 — *"And we know that all things work together for good to those who love God, to those who are the called according to His purpose."*

REFLECT:

Take some time to reflect on this chapter. How has God previously turned pain into purpose in your life? Remember that He can do that again.

REMEMBER:

"No one can predict how God will make it work, especially when life's surprises come our way like losing a loved one suddenly or losing a loved one who died a slow death. It is beyond our limitations; therefore, no one can fathom what God will do from beginning to end. He is the best potter, carpenter, and weaver there is and in the end it is beautiful."

PART II:
BEAUTY FOR ASHES

CHAPTER 4:
THE WILDERNESS OF GRIEF

"When will the pain end?"

After experiencing the suffocating feelings of grief for several years, I started to pick up on its rhythm and routines. One of the things I learned is that it is not a linear process at all.

As I imagined how grief felt for me and probably for a lot of other people, I always imagined a wilderness and we will explore that in a bit.

As we enter part II of this book, we will explore what the process of grief can look like from a dual-perspective.

As a **Licensed Clinical Social Worker (LCSW)**, I know the phases of grief from that lens. I have been taught the most common theory, called **DABDA**, originated by Elisabeth Kübler-Ross. She studied the stages of death and dying, and it has been used to describe the stages of grief as well, from a mental health standpoint.

The first phase is described as **denial**, which means the ones grieving the loss may try to avoid the reality that this person is gone or the person themselves could be in denial about their own mortality quickly approaching. I too had moments of denial. I remember calling my dad's old cell phone, thinking maybe he would pick up the phone or maybe he would text back. I knew he was gone, and I also chose to deny it at the same time. The pain was too great, and denial helps you cope with what is while trying to hold onto what was. I still remember his cell phone number by heart **to this day**.

The second stage is **anger**, and most of us know that anger is usually a secondary emotion to something else going on underneath. After further digging and investigating, it may be **buried** pain, hurt, unforgiveness, or resentment lying dormant, and anger is the protective shield we use to escape vulnerability.

In the midst of grief and dying, we can use anger as a way to exert our emotions and feelings. Whether you are the one dying or the one grieving, anger is used to shift the focus off of you and onto something else. We may mask how we really feel with anger because it's **socially** more acceptable than vulnerability. The issue with that is the pain doesn't go away. Anger is often the most ineffective and destructive emotion because it is usually not the original emotion. One can say that anger makes things worse, as you may end up saying or doing something out of this place, which can cause great regret.

Grieving someone can stir up anger, and usually people place that anger toward God. How could God, who is known to be kind and good, allow such things to happen? How could He take my father away, my baby away, or my friend away? Why did this happen?

All of these questions are normal, and it's important that you go to the right source to find the answers. Anger only wants to blame someone or something else, and while it's human to feel an emotion, it isn't effective to act on it (**see Moses in Numbers 20:10-12 acting out of anger**). That same anger can even be displaced onto the one who has gone.

I remember feeling abandoned by my dad because I thought in my mind, "He left me." I struggled with him saying, "I'm ready to go home," because I felt like he gave up. I was angry with him for leaving me to fend for myself. I was angry with him for not being here to walk me down the aisle, to see his future grandbabies, or to allow me to take care of him as he took care of me.

Anger only pointed at myself and based my grief on my selfish needs and wants. I later realized transitioning on was about him and God. God called him home and he was ready. I was angry with God too, but I later realized God gives and He takes away — and who am I to question that? He and my dad had already reconciled that decision. It was his time.

This points me to Paul in Philippians 1, when he shares being hard pressed between the two; whether to stay for the furtherance of his ministry or to be with Christ which is far better.

I am not sure if my father had a conversation with God in this context, but when he said "I am ready to go home" we all knew what he meant. Though I was mad at him for that, I now understand that was the better choice anyways.

The third phase is **bargaining**. This is where one might think they have control. We think if we do something or make a deal, it will bring our loved one back or keep us alive. But the hard truth is, we do not control our time here on earth, nor do we control someone else's.

This phase causes you to find false hope and dwell on the "should've, would've, and could-haves." It comes from a place of desperation and a willingness to try everything within our power to bring our loved one back, live longer, or ease the pain quicker.

I don't recall ever bargaining during my own time of grief, but I know how desperate I felt to do anything to take the pain away. I tried different vices to cope—and most of them were not healthy but were a quick fix for the deep pain. Bargaining isn't realistic with grief, loss, or death, but it gives us some **illusory** sense of control. The truth is, we have none. And that alone is a hard reality to accept.

The fourth phase is **depression**. Most of us know what depression is and/or have felt similar symptoms that come with it. It's an appropriate response to loss, death, and grief. It's okay to feel sad and miss the person you have lost. It's okay to mourn the fact that you may be dying. It's okay to feel all these things as we've seen illustrated in the Bible time after time.

God doesn't want us to numb our feelings, He wants to take care of them. God made us with the ability to feel things fluidly, and at times, we get stuck there. So, in this stage, it's important to use the right resources, people, and the Word of

God to help strengthen you, so that you do not get stuck in a cycle of depression. My years of depression went undiagnosed and unknown. I later discovered I was depressed, and I got the help I needed.

We must remember that the Word of God brings healing to our minds, emotions, and souls.

Psalm 23:4 is a great reminder of God's comfort

> *"Even though I walk through the darkest valley of death, I will fear no evil, for You are with me; Your rod and Your staff, they comfort me."* (Psalm 23:4)

Lastly, **acceptance** is known as the fifth and final phase of grief from a theoretical lens. This stage is where one gets to the place of accepting life as it is without the person you lost. This is where you acknowledge that their life is no longer on this side of eternity.

You get to a place of living with this grief even if you don't approve of it. You don't have to approve of something to accept it, but life does move on. And it hurts how quickly life keeps going when your life stops in its tracks due to a devastating loss.

Accepting is realizing that you will still have moments. You will still cry. You will still miss the person. You will still mourn what was.

Acceptance is not letting go—it is moving forward with them in your heart instead.

After sharing the five phases of death, dying, and grief, I want you to **shift now to** a spiritual lens. As believers, we may experience these phases, but we often go about them differently. I have my own idea of what the grief journey may look like from a believer's standpoint, based on my personal experiences.

I want to note that not all phases have to be experienced, and the grief process is not linear as I said before. I personally call the grief process **"a wilderness,"** and at times, there are pit stops along the way. But before we discuss those pit stops or phases, let's explore what a wilderness is.

A wilderness is defined as an uncultivated, uninhabited, and inhospitable region. It is uncharted territory with no straight & narrow path to follow.

Spiritually, a wilderness is often symbolic of a desolate place, where faith, character, and your spiritual life is refined as God calls you to a place of complete reliance on Him. It can often feel very isolating and a state of solitude.

Given how isolating grief can be at times, it is easy to see how this overlaps with going into a spiritual wilderness. Grief doesn't just impact your physical life and emotions, it impacts your spirit too. Grief often draws you into a place of solitude and recovery, without any script, rulebook, or procedure.

In a wilderness, you may picture trees, an unmarked path, and a place that is often neglected or abandoned. A wilderness is indeed a desolate place and grief can feel like that.

As I mentioned in a previous chapter, after a while, everyone and everything becomes very quiet after you lose someone. People stop acknowledging that you are still grieving.

Personally, I believe that grief actually doesn't start when you lose someone; it starts **after you bury them.**

It didn't really hit me until the nurses came in and took my cold baby away from me when it was time for discharge. It didn't really hit me until I saw my dad's casket going into the ground. It didn't really hit me until my phone went silent, and I was at home no longer hearing his footsteps or experiencing my baby kick me in the morning.

Loss is the event but grief waits for the silence. Grief is messy, desolate, lonely, abandoned, and clearly not a place many voluntarily journey through. Grief is a wilderness.

In the Bible, we see wildernesses many times.

We see Hagar and Ishmael journey into a wilderness in Genesis 21:14, where the Lord still met them there. God provided for Hagar and Ishmael in the wilderness.

You see God leading His people by way of a wilderness in Exodus 13:18-21. He even went before them by day in a pillar of cloud and by night in a pillar of fire. When there was no water and the people of Israel began to complain, God provided a well of water after Moses cried out (Exodus 15). Again, the Lord provided and was with them.

Or what about David in the wilderness, escaping Saul (1 Samuel 24:14), where Saul's own son, Jonathan, sought David out, protected him, and strengthened him in God? Even then, God provided protection and mild companionship in the wilderness.

Or what about the mighty Elijah fleeing to the wilderness after being threatened by Jezebel and pleading that God take his life because his emotions were overwhelming him? Even then, God sent him an angel to give him food for strength.

Or what about John the Baptist in Matthew 3 preparing the way of the Lord and preaching in the wilderness, making the path straight in an unmarked, uncharted territory?

Or what about our very own Savior, Jesus Christ, being led into the wilderness (Matthew 4:1), where He was tempted by Satan?

I think you get my drift now.

The wilderness has often been used in Scripture to represent a place where God takes His people to be pruned, refined, and ultimately to need Him more than anything else. He always meets His people in the wilderness.

I can't imagine the wildlife living in the wilderness — and I can't imagine the temptations that come with thinking God has left us there to die. Yet we see, time after time, that God provided a well of water, bread from heaven, or an escape.

God is in every wilderness.

The world itself was made from a void, an unformed wilderness (Genesis 1:2), so who better to hold onto in the wilderness of grief than the God who formed the world from it?

There are many trials and temptations that can exist in a wilderness. Refinement is not an easy process, and God purposefully and kindly causes us to go without so that we can fully depend on Him.

At some point, or many points in life, believers must go through a wilderness process. We often try to avoid these seasons because we don't want to step into the unknown. But Jesus Christ was led into the wilderness. It wasn't voluntary.

And in the wilderness, He used the Word of God as He responded to the enemy's temptations.

Submitting your life to God's perfect will means yielding to His plan and process, which almost certainly includes a wilderness season.

Grief is not a voluntary wilderness season, but many of us have been led there by force. Many of you are there now.

But God. But God is so kind and gracious that He goes before us. Even though the wilderness seems untouched, God has already been there. He prepared that place for you (Revelation 12:6) and for me, regardless of the reason or circumstance.

In every wilderness, God provides the shelter, food, and security we need. In Hosea 2:14, it is written that God leads us into the wilderness and speaks to us tenderly there.

Jesus describes Himself as gentle and humble at heart (Matthew 11:29). A wilderness is a place to hear God clearly — not to tune Him out.

If we can't know who God is in the wilderness, how will we recognize and hear Him in the Promised Land?

The wilderness is nature's finest habitat. There are no distractions. There are no more phone calls or check-ins.

This is where you learn God's voice. This is where you learn God's nature. This is where you are prepared for what's next.

Think about the wildernesses of Moses, Joseph, and David. The wisdom, strength, and power formed there made them victorious in the end.

No one is writing "enter the wilderness" on their calendar, but I bet you we're all trying to write out "exit the wilderness." That is not always the case, sadly.

The wilderness is where your pain, idols, disloyalty, and false narratives of God are revealed. Grief is an interesting, uncomfortable way to expose those things, especially through the clinical-based phases I described before.

Remember, in the previous chapter, my grief exposed so many other issues I already had which is why my process was so long. God is not in the business of drive by services, if you want full healing and restoration, go into the wilderness.

Anger at God reveals disbelief in who God is. Denial and bargaining reveal control issues that require deliverance and restoration. Depression reveals the pain you need healing for. Acceptance reveals the mercy and grace you need to move forward.

It is in this wilderness where you have intimate moments with God and move from just knowing Him as your Master to knowing Him as your Friend, your Bridegroom, and your Redeemer.

This season can prepare you for what's ahead if you allow it to.

I emphasize the notion that you have to allow this wilderness of grief (or any other wilderness) to be God-kept and Spirit-driven. It is a choice. We do have free will.

You must sense, decide, and know that God is with you, just as illustrated in the Bible.

The same God and Spirit who led the Israelites into the wilderness in the Old Testament is the same God and Spirit who led Jesus Christ into the wilderness in the Gospels.

If you remain unaware of this, it will be easy to miss what God is doing and fall into temptation.

The Israelites complained and complained (Exodus 17), and God still remained faithful.

Don't allow your human eye, mind, and hunger to fall into the enemy's lies and traps during this time.

As I said in previous chapters, you have two choices when you are in a desolate place: You can rely on yourself... Or you can rely on God. You can rely on pain or God's promises and purposes. You decide at the crossroads.

So again, grief is a wilderness to me. It's messy, uncomfortable, unknown, and often avoided.

It is easy to lose hope here. It is easy to be caught up in the what-ifs.

But this is God's perfect canvas for the masterpiece He is making (Ephesians 2:10), so that we can continue to do the good works He predestined long ago... even in our grief.

Trust me, I know it's hard. I know it gets lonely. And it's okay to keep casting this heavy burden, the care of grief, on Him (1 Peter 5:7).

But I also know that God can make all things new, even in the wake of death. Because God is greater than grief.

DEVOTIONAL REFLECTION

READ:

1 Peter 5:7 — *"Cast all your cares on Him because He cares for you."*

REFLECT:

Take some time to reflect on this chapter. Which stage of grief are you at? Is God calling you into a wilderness?

REMEMBER:

"The wilderness is where your pain, idols, disloyalty, and false narratives of God are revealed."

CHAPTER 5:
WITH GOD

"This all seems unfixable."

The main thing people will say is that grief is multifaceted, and **they're right**. The narrative of grief is filled with sorrow, desolation, and anguish. It has a doom-and-gloom aura that can dictate how you process that grief. That very same narrative plays a role in how we see God in the midst of our grief. Many of us may have developed a new narrative that says "God didn't love me.", or "God heals His favorites.", or "God isn't good to me." similar to what I thought in my quote at the beginning of this chapter.

This isn't something you just pray away, **especially when** grief is all over the Bible.

We see grief throughout Scripture:

- David weeping over the death of his son (2 Samuel 12:15-23).
- Job tearing his robe, shaving his head, and falling to the ground in worship after losing all ten of his children (Job 1:20).
- Mary and Martha mourning their brother Lazarus, and Jesus Himself weeping (John 11:33-35).
- Naomi grieving the loss of her husband and sons, saying, *"Call me Mara, because the Almighty has made my life very bitter"* (Ruth 1:20).
- Even Paul expresses *"great sorrow and unceasing anguish"* for his people (Romans 9:2).
- Elisha tears his clothes in sorrow after seeing his mentor Elijah taken up (2 Kings 2:12)

There is weeping, there is mourning, and there is also some version of acceptance to move forward. There is no "correct" or "right" way to grieve, and most people promote the idea of grieving however you want. While I agree with that, I also want to challenge it. As a believer, there is a way to grieve—though it will look different for each person. The major difference in how we grieve, as believers, is this: **we grieve with God.** Not from God. Not away from God. **But with God.**

Anytime life events happen, especially those on either end of the spectrum (life and death), we bring God's name up.

"Oh thank God for our bundle of joy."

"Oh thank God he/she died a believer."

"He/She is in a better place and resting with God."

"Why would God allow this?"

"Is God really who He says He is when this person died so young?"

And so forth.

We tend to associate God with either side of the spectrum because we believe (I hope) that He is ruler of both. That is true. And the same way we identify God as good when we give birth to our baby or celebrate new life is the same way we need to identify God as good when our loved one passes.

If we truly believe that God is indeed ruler over both, then we need to walk with Him in both. From birth, after a child comes into the world, we need God's counsel and wisdom to raise that child—not just parents, culture, or society. Your village is important, but God is more important when it comes to stewarding parenthood.

Similarly, when someone leaves this world, we still need God's counsel and wisdom on how to navigate grief, not just people, friends, and family. Your village is important, but God is more important when it comes to plowing through the thickness of grief.

But I've learned and experienced that when it comes to negative circumstances such as loss and grief, it's easier to question God and challenge His character than it is to walk through it with Him.

Let's not get it twisted… Grief is hard. And we're human. The hurt, the pain, the questions, they're all normal. The healing has to take place. The tears must fall. The thoughts must be revived. But all of that can be done **with Him.**

Just because you are without your loved one doesn't mean you are without God, Jesus Christ, or the Holy Spirit. The Triune God is there, all three in one, to cover you. You need to go through this with Him.

You may be asking now, "Okay, Lisa, how does one do this grief journey *with* God?

I'm so glad you asked. Let's discuss:

Knowledge → Perspective → Action

1. KNOWLEDGE → *Knowing* who God is in grief.

The first step to managing grief with God is by knowing who God is. The Bible says, *"My people are destroyed for lack of knowledge"* (Hosea 4:6). We have many believers who lack the knowledge about God that they need to navigate life. You have many believers living a dead life because they lack the source of it. The Bible says, *"The Word of God is living and active"* (Hebrews 4:12), which means to live a full life, you need to know your Word.

John 1:1 declares, *"In the beginning was the Word, and the Word was with God, and the Word was God."* So as you know the Word, you get to know God, and you get to know Christ your Savior like never before. Jesus came to give life more abundantly, so in His Word, wrapped in His flesh, He is giving you life — His life.

So if you don't know God and His Word, how can you possibly acknowledge who He truly is without an influencer on Instagram telling you, or your pastor reminding you, or your family and friends affirming it for you?

You need to know who God is for yourself. Even in the face of death, loss, and grief, you can declare:

God is good.
God is kind.
God is merciful.

God is Elohim.
God is Yahweh.
God is Adonai.

God is unchangeable.

He is a comforter.
He is sovereign.
He is who He is (I AM) regardless of life's circumstances.

Testify about Him.
In the pain, declare who He is.
In the hurt, declare His name.

It will ache your flesh, but with the Truth, the Word, and the Holy Spirit, you can and will overcome it by the declaration from your lips. This is where the Word has to trump feelings. What you say about God during this time is imperative. Do not allow grief to recreate who God is. Do not allow yourself to make grief an idol, that's become a god to you by reshaping and rewriting your very being and future.

You control the narrative by knowing who God is in grief. So, every step of the way, have the attributes of God in your pocket.

2. PERSPECTIVE → Knowing God is *greater* than grief.

Secondly, knowing who God is means we know that **He is greater than death, the grave, and loss. This also means He has greater in store.** For a believer, death is victory. Death is not the end for a believer. There is something greater to look forward to—**eternity.** As we get to know God, we also have a reassurance of our future hope. Jesus Himself says that He is going to prepare a place for us (John 14:2–3). That place is not here on earth. That place is in heaven—a forever home—where pain, sorrow, and tears do not exist.

In Revelation, it says, *"He will wipe every tear from their eyes. There will be no more death or mourning or crying or pain..."* (Revelation 21:4). That is something to give God praise for.

If your loved one died in Christ, **they are in bliss forever.** And even though I know how convincing grief can be when it makes you feel like the walls are closing in and your heart is shattered into pieces, this is not to minimize your pain. This is to hold your pain up to a GREAT God. His greatness is unsearchable (Psalm 145:3).

God is not just looking at our lives here on earth, our lives, as believers, go beyond into eternity with Him, which was His initial design and plan before sin corrupted the earth.

So as you navigate grief, remember His attributes, and also remember His great power.

When you look up the word "great", it is defined as intensity considerably above the average or normal.

The God who brought forth the entire world in Genesis can navigate grief with you. This same great God is abundant in power, The God of gods, Lord of lords, King Eternal, and is the Creator of the ends of the earth (Psalm 147:5, Deuteronomy 10:17-18, 1 Timothy 1:17, Isaiah 40:28). The God who parted the Red Sea for Israel's deliverance (Exodus 14:21-22). The God who was the fourth man in the fire (Daniel 3:25) and shut the mouths of lions (Daniel 6:22). The God whose greatness is described in Isaiah 40 through nature.

There is no excuse but to see His invisible, great qualities since creation (Romans 1:20).

Indeed, **He is a really great God.** His life proves it, and His death and resurrection defeated it.

> *"He disarmed the powers and authorities and made a public spectacle of them, triumphing over them by the cross."* (Colossians 2:15)

> *"That I may know Him and the power of His resurrection and the fellowship of His sufferings..."* (Philippians 3:10)

So, don't pray your grief away — grieve *with* your great God. He is able to meet us in our grief while giving us the reassurance that He has greater in store for our lives on earth, and on the other side of eternity.

And if that loved one was not in Christ, then sadly, there is grief associated with that too. That is very painful. Because as believers, we know there are two places to end up, both being very real. Heaven is real. Hell is real too.

If your loved one was not a believer, **I pray that God captures your heart** as it wanders, as it grieves for their soul, and as it processes the truth.

I know this part is a hard pill to swallow for many — but it is the truth. We can't discuss grief, loss, death, and our eternal destination without acknowledging who God is, reflecting on His greatness, and understanding that there are two places where people end up.

We get to decide… today.

Pause here and ask yourself, *"am I saved?"* If not, here is a verse and a prayer to pray now to secure your salvation for free:

> *"If you confess with your mouth, 'Jesus is Lord,' and believe in your heart that God raised Him from the dead, you will be saved."* (Romans 10:9)

Salvation Prayer

Lord Jesus, I acknowledge I am a sinner. I believe You died for me and rose again and ascended into heaven. I confess You as my Lord and Savior. Come into my heart. Save me. I surrender my life to You. Amen.

Okay, I needed to pause and give space for that because I felt it necessary to discuss that here.

Knowing God is greater, we must also confront the fact that God allows things to happen. Is it always fair to our carnal eyes? **No.**

I mean, how do we address:

- You're omnipotent, so You could have stopped it.
- You're omnipresent, so You were there and still allowed it.
- You're omniscient, so You knew this would happen.

There are truly some things we will never understand on this side.

There are questions you have that this book will not answer—because I can't. There are things our human minds can't wrap around, and fortunately, **this limitation protects us.**

> *"'For My thoughts are not your thoughts, neither are your ways My ways,' declares the Lord."* (Isaiah 55:8-9)

Some things have to go into that "I don't know" file, as I heard my Bishop once say. But just because you don't know everything **does not** mean you don't know God.

This is where you **continue to see Him for who He is.**

Your emotions, flesh, and mind will try to persuade you otherwise, but regardless of our circumstances, *"Jesus Christ is the same yesterday and today and forever"* (Hebrews 13:8).

Let **the Word** answer your questions and regulate your feelings:

When sadness comes, declare:

"The LORD is gracious and compassionate, slow to anger and rich in love." (Psalm 145:8)

When shame and guilt comes, declare:

"You, O Lord, are a shield about me, my glory, and the lifter of my head" (Psalm 3:3)

When second-guessing comes, declare:

"Your word is a lamp to my feet and a light to my path" (Psalm 119:105)

When confusion and inner turmoil comes, declare:

"The peace of God, which transcends all understanding, will guard your hearts and your minds in Christ Jesus." (Philippians 4:7)

When the Word doesn't "feel" like it's working, declare that is. **Grief is foggy**, and we need God to illuminate the way– His Word is the entrance to light. (Psalm 119:130). **And that is the answer.**

If we don't answer these spirals and questions with God's Word, we allow ourselves, our emotions, and the enemy to fill in the blanks. These emotions, if not managed well, become false narratives and can pull us away from the truth.

Yes, **feel your feelings.** But do not let those feelings dictate everything. That requires **surrendering** your emotions too.

I know and remember how many times I've talked to God about losing my dad and baby. I know how deeply I challenged Him and how badly my mind turned against Him when I allowed my emotions to convince me He was not good.

I ended up in **bondage for years.** But glory to God! He set me free. Glory to God—He showed me who He is again and that He is greater than my losses.

If anything, I appreciate God's character more now because **it did not change** toward me even when I changed toward Him.

I was not the Christian who grieved gracefully. I was the believer who thought God did an unkind thing to me. I took it personally. And I had **a lot of unfinished business** with Him.

There was no way I could even be in a place to write this book without dealing with my affliction, my resentment toward God. I had to repent and receive His healing.

When my feelings headed down a rabbit hole, His grace was sufficient. For me to turn around and be where I am today is only **grace.**

I had to repent for my thoughts and my heart posture from that time and refill the voids with His Word. For as it says:

> *"I have hidden your word in my heart that I might not sin against you."* (Psalm 119:11)

In the last chapter, I mentioned it was the Word that had set me free. In this chapter, it is the very same Word that will remind you how *great* God is **when grief makes you forget.**

3. ACTION → *Drawing* **closer to Him through grief.**

Lastly, how to grieve with God is by **drawing closer** to Him. The Word of God says, *"Draw near to God and He will draw near to you"* (James 4:8).

Drawing closer isn't just showing up to church. Drawing closer isn't just looking up another sermon.

Sometimes, drawing near to God is in your quiet place.

You know when a loved one tells you to come closer and they share something so dear, so sweet, and so profound — something so intimate that's just between you two? Let that be your way of drawing closer to God. To talk to God and walk with Him on this journey is an intimate process. **Get personal with Him here.**

Tune out the noise, the people, and the routines, and spend quality time with God. You can do this through worship, prayer and fasting, and taking time to speak in your unknown tongue. You can even do this as you visit your loved one's grave, go to therapy, or seek Pastoral care

Acknowledging who God is and proclaiming His greatness is the way you draw closer.

And yes, you can draw closer to God while in pain. The two don't have to be separated.

This makes me think of Hannah in 1 Samuel. The Message Translation titles this chapter as "Hannah pours out her heart to God." That is a beautiful description of drawing closer.

After years of being barren, mocked, and grieving her unfulfilled desire, she went to God and the Bible says:

"In her deep anguish Hannah prayed to the Lord, weeping bitterly." (1 Samuel 1:10)

Hannah was in deep pain and wept before she made a vow to the Lord. So even in her pain, she drew to God and He drew to her. In that intimate moment, Hannah gives God the very thing she had been praying for.

For me personally, these intimate moments allow us to experience our relationship with God in a different way.

I feel like my perspective on life completely changed after losing two loved ones just 10 days apart. The trauma, the pain, the backsliding, the poor coping, the dysregulated emotions, and healing — piece by piece — have allowed me to see God as a friend.

Not a human friend, but a God who doesn't just sit on a throne looking down, but a God who comes down to sit with me.

A God who gave me a Helper to teach me things my human mind could not comprehend.

A God who gave me a Savior to live life through.

A God who counseled me back to health before I did anything else. He cared more about my heart because out of the heart is where we serve. And to get to this place took a step of faith:

- **By faith**, I can trust that God allowed what He allowed because He is sovereign.
- **By faith**, my story did not end there.
- **By faith**, your story does not end with grief and pain.
- **By faith**, your loved one in Christ's story did not end with death.

I remember holding my baby and my dad, asking God why. I didn't get an answer back. But this time of my life made me ask God more questions than I ever had before. It developed a sense of curiosity in me. I hated the circumstances—but in hindsight, this was used to draw me closer.

By faith, we can draw closer to God—with a veil torn, an altar sacrificed for, a debt paid for, and a wound healed from. It minimizes our circumstances and magnifies Him.

Drawing closer to God does not take away the "why" questions immediately. Drawing closer to God will not answer all of your questions deeply. Drawing closer to God will not take away all the feelings. But it will give you the arsenal to move forward.

It is in the secret place of God where you find the strength to accept and move on.

After Hannah's prayer and vow to the Lord, after she wept inconsolably, the Lord did not give her an answer right away. However, the Bible says:

> *"...then went her way and ate something, and her face was no longer downcast."* (1 Samuel 1:18)

She remembered who God is, she knew He is greater by identifying Him as Lord of Hosts Almighty God, and she drew closer in vulnerability, humility, and surrender. Her first response was to pray to the Lord as a coping strategy amidst her deep anguish.

After David lost his son, the Bible says:

> *"Then David got up from the ground. After he had washed, put on lotions and changed his clothes, he went into the house of the Lord and worshiped. Then he went to his own house, and at his request they served him food, and he ate."* (2 Samuel 12:20)

David, after fasting and praying that God would spare his son, went to the house of the Lord to **worship after hearing his son died**. David had to have remembered who God was, remembered God is greater, and through worship he drew closer to God.

How many of us, like me, would have probably strayed from God and blamed Him? But here we have Biblical examples of people experiencing real sorrow, anguish, and pain and **yet their faith in God overcame their feelings.** The same God who allowed these things to occur was the same God who gave them the strength to move forward, comforting them every step of the way. What a **GREAT** God we serve!

As we close this chapter, I want you to remember that He steps into our areas of pain, lifts it up from our hands, and propels us forward. That is navigating grief *with* God. And just as multifaceted as grief is, God is also **multifaceted,** and that is greater than any nuance or facet of grief. If you don't know… **then draw into Him to find out.**

DEVOTIONAL REFLECTION

READ:

James 4:8 — *"Draw near to God and He will draw near to you."*

REFLECT:

Take some time to reflect on this chapter. How can you draw closer to God in your grief?

REMEMBER:

"The major difference in how we grieve, as believers, is this: we grieve with God. Not from God. Not away from God. But with God."

CHAPTER 6:
JOB'S BLUEPRINT

"Where were you when I was in need?"

One of the things people are often afraid of is questioning God when facing grief. It's difficult, especially as a believer, to be upset or angry with God without feeling like you are committing blasphemy.

But one of the books in the Bible that profoundly depicts human nature and God's sovereignty while facing intense suffering is the book of Job.

In this chapter, we'll see Job's humanity and calamity, which ended with God's sovereignty and restoration. It's important that we connect with people in the Bible because oftentimes, we can feel as though the Bible is out of touch with our reality and that is far from the truth.

Like you, like me, this man went through it, yet he remained faithful to God. What I love the most is **his display of** raw emotion. Even though he remained faithful to God, that did not mean he didn't ask questions, seek counsel, or feel the pain associated with the events that occurred.

Job confronted God and wanted to understand why certain things happened. He went through the internal conflict between his emotions and the truth of who God is which can relate to most if not all of us.

In **Job 10**, Job speaks of his soul loathing his life and pleads that God does not oppress or condemn him. This connects with anyone who has experienced loss and starts to hate their life, while hoping that God does not chastise them for it.

As the chapters go on, you read how his friends respond, how his wife responds, and then you see Job beginning to trust God but there was a long process to get to that point.

In **Job 13:15**, Job says, "Though He slay me, yet will I trust Him." I don't think Job meant that God was intentionally slaying him, but **that He is** allowing life's circumstances to happen and he proclaims his trust in Him amidst it all.

We also see in **Job 7:20**, him asking God what he has done to become God's target. These two separate scriptures indicate the conflict Job was experiencing. On one end Job trusted God and on the other end Job was boldly taking what occurred personally — like many of us would have.

This describes human nature at its best. Living in this carnal body will give room for opposing thoughts, questions, or feelings to arise — yet even still, we have to trust God in our hearts and with our mouths.

It's so easy to use God as a punching bag when life gets hard and circumstances like death occur. We feel like it's so unfair and we somehow got the short end of the stick. I remember feeling envious anytime someone said they received healing from the Lord, because my father didn't. I took things personally too.

We often change our demeanor and narrative about God when we suffer. It can become a dark tunnel with no sight of light. But I encourage all of us to use Job as an example. In **Job** 26 and 27, Job declares God's majesty and maintains his integrity. Though he endured many losses back-to-back, he still proclaims, "My lips will not speak wickedness, nor my tongue utter deceit" **(Job 27:4)**.

He held onto his righteousness. He did not allow his circumstances to dictate his ending though I am sure it was tempting to do so. His own wife told him to curse God and die. And like Job's wife, many people lose their faith when navigating loss. They may not explicitly say they're done with God, but in their hearts, they may be.

We all have to take a deeper look at our hearts and ask ourselves:

> "What is my heart saying about God through this situation?"

> "What is it saying about me?"

This is the moment you allow God to examine you and search you.

When I began to take a deeper look into myself, I realized my heart was angry with God for years after my losses. I stopped believing He was good and that lie from hell turned into a web of many other lies that followed me for years. It brainwashed me to believe that God had it out for me. It took wise counsel, the Word of God, prayer, and deliverance to break me free.

I remember sitting in my room, weeping, and telling God how I truly felt. Once I was able to expose the dirty lies within my heart, I felt free to move forward and trust Him again with the pieces of my heart that were damaged. He already knew how I felt, but something about uttering the words — exposing the lies and being real with God —- set me free.

It's important to be honest, not religious. It's important to bring these things to God like Job did, not avoid it. So stop pretending to be okay when God knows you are not. He knows grief can feel like a trial, tribulation, and a test all at once.

After getting through the rough trial-like years of my own grief, I remember someone from church told me, *"God knew He could trust you with this testimony."* I've always sat with that. While God does not oppress His children, He knows oppression will happen because we live in a fallen world. Yet, even in that, He equips our faith to endure which transforms into a testimony.

I admire that about Job. He didn't hide his feelings, he confronted them and respectfully brought them to the throne, which ultimately led to a beautiful testimony of restoration.

That moment of weeping, questioning, and raw honesty turned into a moment of redefining who God is for me. That moment opened the door to true healing and freedom. And it opened my heart to hear what He had to say too.

One thing you must know is that God is always speaking and just as we come to Him with our grief, pain, and questions, He will answer. I love Job chapters 38-41 because this is where God answers Job. He didn't answer why these things happened, He answered with His omnipotence.

God tells Job to prepare himself like a man and get ready to answer Him. Then, He begins to ask:

"Where were you when I laid the foundations of the earth?" (Job 38:4)

"Who determined its measurements?" (Job 38:5)

"Have you commanded the morning since your days began, and caused the dawn to know its place?" (Job 38:12)

"Have the gates of death been revealed to you?" (Job 38:17)

"Do you know it, because you were born then, or because the number of your days is great?" (Job 38:21)

"Have you entered the treasury of snow, or have you seen the treasury of hail, which I have reserved for the time of trouble, for the day of battle and war?" (Job 38:22-23)

"Who has put wisdom in the mind? Or who has given understanding to the heart?" (Job 38:36)

"Does the eagle mount up at your command, and make its nest on high?" (Job 39:27)

"Shall the one who contends with the Almighty correct Him?" (Job 40:2)

"Do you have an arm like God? Or can you thunder with a voice like His?" (Job 40:9)

After God questions Job, Job responds:

"Behold, I am vile; what shall I answer You? I lay my hand over my mouth." (Job 40:4, NKJV)

I only included a few verses from these chapters, but as you can see, God had to remind Job who He was, is, and will forever be. It felt like a parent telling their child "Do you know who you are speaking to?"

And that was the answer to Job's calamity — **it was God's sovereignty.** It was God's perfect wisdom. It was God's unfathomable ways and plans.

I don't think it was ever Job's purest intention to question God's might. But like Job, sometimes we fall into that trap.

Sometimes, we bring God too far down to our human level, and He is not like us. Sometimes, when we go through things, we lose our fear, trembling, and reverence for God. But God is God. We can't demand answers from God with our limited human understanding. Instead, we have to cling to God above all else because His ways are higher. And regardless of what happens or who we lose, He remains that way.

The book of Job really humbled me. Even with my own issues, I remember God speaking something similar to me.

"What now, Lisa?" God said to me.

As in, what am I to do now? Knowing that I have endured losses... that I have felt depressed, lonely, confused, and angry... but is this how it ends? They are not coming back so what now?

Is this who I will decide to be? Is this how I will continue to define God?

This is another moment where I had to choose to see God greater than my grief, just like Job did. I had to close my mouth and revere Him anew.

I had to let go of being a victim to grief. It is in this place where God was magnified in all His authority and might and my grief now had a place to rest. There is a **boundary** between our experiences and God's infinite ways.

This is where we find our peace. This is where our faith is strengthened. This is where we are reminded of our place. And that's where we lay down and surrender our grief.

We surrender it to God *"to whom everything under heaven belongs"* (Job 41:11, NLT), **even death.**

Restoration from Job

After this journey with God, Job came back to what he knew was true about God. Despite what he went through, he remained steadfast in his belief in who God is.

Not only did he hear God — he saw God. He repents in Job chapter 42, and God identifies that Job has spoken of Him what is right, whereas Job's friends did not. Job then turns his eye off of himself and prays for his friends. We read and witness the Lord accepting Job and restoring his losses, **blessing his latter days more than his beginning.**

> *"And the Lord restored Job's losses when he prayed for his friends. Indeed the Lord gave Job twice as much as he had before."* (Job 42:10)

> *"Now the Lord blessed the latter days of Job more than his beginning."* (Job 42:12)

In the end, look at how faithful God was to Job in restoring him. He is the same yesterday, today, and forevermore (Hebrews 13:8). So, if He did it for Job, He can do it for you. I know He certainly has done it for me.

Though losing my father and my baby boy were the hardest things I've ever experienced, God restored my heart. And not just a heart for myself, but a heart enlarged for others who are grieving too.

These restoration outcomes look different for everyone, **but God knows who needs what.** He knows how hard grief is. He knows how many people have questioned Him and strayed away from Him because of it. Yet, He wants to be invited into this deep place to restore it. So, don't waste the rest of your days contending with God about the sad and the inevitable things in life when you can spend your days living restored.

In closing, unfortunately this side of eternity will come with a lot of suffering which is a part of grief. Job was this chapter's example of someone who experienced deep suffering, but there are many more who suffered in the Bible. There's Daniel who was sent into exile in Babylon (Daniel 1) or Joseph who endured betrayal, slavery, and imprisonment (Genesis 37, 39). Still we see how God allowed suffering—yet they remained faithful because they knew God was greater. And in the end what was meant for evil, God intended it for good (Genesis 50:20).

This isn't just Job's blueprint. This is God's blueprint on how He works it all out for our good, according to His purpose. This is the blueprint we all ought to follow.

DEVOTIONAL REFLECTION

READ:

Job 13:15 – *"Though he slay me, yet will I trust in him…"*

REFLECT:

Take some time to reflect on this chapter. How has the Book of Job confronted some of the questions you have about your calamity and grief?

REMEMBER:

"The answer to Job's calamity was God's sovereignty. It was God's perfect wisdom. It was God's unfathomable ways and plans."

CHAPTER 7:
THE END OF OLD, THE BEGINNING OF NEW

"Everyone has forgotten about them and I am all alone."

One of the beautiful things I had with my experience of loss and grief is **time**. I couldn't see it that way until a few years ago, honestly. But I started to realize that many people lose loved ones very suddenly. Many people did not get the opportunity to see their loved one transition.

I had my baby boy in my belly for five months, so I got to know him through the ultrasounds, my pictures, and his kicks that woke me up in the morning. I got to hold him and see his beautiful face when I gave birth to him. I got to name him and fill out a birth and death certificate, which at the time was very traumatic. **But now, I appreciate that.** Many women experience a miscarriage or preterm birth, and they are not able to have that same experience to hold onto.

With my father, he battled cancer for about three years. There were ups and downs, but he always remained consistent. He never used his sickness as an excuse. He still worked full-time, picked me up from school, cooked, and participated in everything we did as a family, until he was physically unable to.

That's why I call him my hero. And thankfully, due to the Holy Spirit's nudge, I was able to come home early from my internship to make sure I said goodbye and "I love you" before he transitioned.

My father's cancer was a dangerous, sneaky one—one that typically does not give even a year of life after diagnosis. But glory to God, he lived for three years with it. Even the surgeon was shocked. God's mercy gave my father and our family extra time.

I didn't know how fast death would come one day, but I am thankful that it was slow over the years of his sickness. I am thankful we had time together to talk about things, share memories, and document his journey. I am thankful I got to see him right before he transitioned. I am thankful he transitioned at home, as he wanted to.

I recognize many people weren't able to have as much time with the person they lost. Some people lost a loved one suddenly, some people didn't get a chance to say goodbye, and some people don't have any memories to hold onto. We all have different points of view but prayerfully, we can all be encouraged from the same Source. Here's a few messages to those experiencing grief from a different angle.

To those who have lost someone suddenly:

I have never experienced that with a family member, but I have with friends. It is unimaginable to see someone in the morning and hear of their passing that same night.

If you are reading this after experiencing a sudden loss, my heart goes out to you. I pray that God's love reaches every piece of pain you're experiencing. Regardless of death being delayed or sudden—it hurts. But the impact and trauma of a sudden death is one I empathize with.

We see Jacob mourning the misperceived tragic loss of his son Joseph and he was deep in the sorrow to the point where he could not be consoled (Genesis 37:34-35). The shock of a sudden death is hard for anyone to bear since no one knows when their time has come (Ecclesiastes 9:12).

It may seem like nothing will fix it, nothing will cure it, but I know that the Lord who made the heavens can help you cope with this tragic, sudden shift in your life.

The Lord will help you in time of need.

> *"I will lift up my eyes to the hills — From whence comes my help? My help comes from the Lord, Who made heaven and earth."* Psalm 121:1-2

> *"I cried to the LORD with my voice, And He heard me from His holy hill. Selah"* Psalm 3:4

To those with complicated grief:

Maybe you have lost someone who has hurt you, abused you, or mistreated you. And sadly, grief still comes. But there are often conflicting emotions attached, which requires deep heart surgery and a time of prolonged recovery.

No one wants to say this out loud, but part of you may even feel relieved that they are gone. These are the hard truths we must confront in grief. If we don't, they can eat us alive.

Complicated grief can become a cancer for many; the bitterness, the anger, the shame, the guilt, the flashbacks of the pain the person caused you can become a stronghold. Honestly, the best thing I can encourage you to do — if you have unresolved or conflicting feelings about the person who passed — is to voluntarily admit yourself into God's surgery room. Go to Him with **vulnerability, honesty, and humility.**

Similar to most surgeries, you need to go "under". You need to be under anesthesia and allow God to expose, cut, remove, repair, and replace your heart, renew your mind, and restore your soul before you can fully recover. I personally know people who have sought deliverance for unresolved grief and unforgiveness — this is for you to move on.

> *"He leads us besides still waters, He restores our souls for His name's sake. Yea, though I walk through the valley of the shadow of death, I will fear no evil: for thou art with me; thy rod and thy staff they comfort me"* (Psalm 23: 2-4).

In this place, **God is not only your surgeon, He is your Shepherd.** And before you can move on, you need to lie down, lay down your pride, willfulness, and resentment because a heart that harbors resentment produces nothing and could lead to your own destruction (Job 36:13-16).

Another thing I encourage you to do is, seek therapy or grief counseling.

Those issues in your heart need to be processed. And God can absolutely do that—but He's also equipped counselors to walk with us through it too.

I did grief counseling after my father passed. Not because of him necessarily, but because I had unresolved feelings about my family in general. I felt like my father abandoned me, and that opened up many other cans of pain. But addressing it was necessary for my recovery and for moving forward.

Though your loved one has passed on, the issues and emotions you carry are no longer theirs, **they're yours to deal with.**

Brushing it aside with blanket phrases won't fix it. Grief can unearth past wounds and bring up emotions that don't feel godly. And **God is mighty to save you through it all.**

Don't allow the enemy to shame, guilt or weaponize your pain against you. I've seen how the enemy will bring up those nasty past memories to make you grieve painfully instead of purposefully. He doesn't care about your healing. He wants you to stay stuck, miserable, and conflicted, which can ultimately draw you away from God even further.

So it's your responsibility to take that pain to the Cross. You do this through prayer, worship, the Word of God, and accessing support or counseling along the way. Let Jesus Himself:

- Heal you from what that person did to you.
- Heal you from the ache of their passing.
- Heal you from the mental replay of painful memories—so you can move on.

It all begins in God's surgery room. And it all continues by renewing your mind daily.

The same way we follow post operative instructions to maintain our healing after surgery, is the same way you need the Word of God to daily renew your mind after heart surgery.

Your deliverance can be maintained.

"He heals the brokenhearted and binds up their wounds." (Psalm 147:3)

"And do not be conformed to this world, but be transformed by the renewing of your mind, that you may prove what is that good and acceptable and perfect will of God." (Romans 12:2)

"You are my hiding place; you will protect me from trouble and surround me with songs of deliverance." (Psalm 32:7)

To those who were caregivers:

My prayer is that God gives you strength as you grieve.

There is often a strange mixture of ease and grief after the person you cared for passes. And there's also honor in that. I pray you use this time to refill your cup. Refresh the parts of your life that were placed on the back burner because you took on the sacred task of caregiving in someone's final days, months, or years. I can only imagine the reward awaiting you.

This is no easy task. And my prayer is that during this time of moving forward, you get back to what once brought you joy.

May the joy of the Lord give you strength (Nehemiah 8:10). May you reclaim time by immersing yourself into the things you love, fellowshipping with those who rejuvenate you in your community, and thanking God for the grace He lavished on you to care for your loved one.

Your labor of love was not in vain. This is for my mom too.

> *"You make known to me the path of life; you will fill me with joy in your presence, with eternal pleasures at your right hand."* (Psalm 16:11)
>
> *"You have turned my mourning into joyful dancing. You have taken away my clothes of mourning and clothed me with joy."* (Psalm 30:11)
>
> *"He will once again fill your mouth with laughter and your lips with shouts of joy."* (Job 8:21)

I covered quite a few differing positions of grief, and I am sure there are many more. There's also grief over pets, opportunities, heartbreaks, and what could have been. While all of these are not covered in this book, the same scriptures, prayers, and words of wisdom apply.

So When the End Comes, What Happens After?

Depending on the type of loss it will dictate what happens next. Typically there are a lot of family dynamics that start to arise. I have noticed that deep, hidden family dynamics come up to the surface at the time of birth and the time of death. It could be a really positive experience or a really negative one.

Another thing to consider is how each person was related to the person who has died. Losing a spouse versus losing a parent is different. Losing a child versus losing a sibling is different. And while this isn't the time to compare the size, weight, or shape of each other's grief, it is important to note that it will be different for everyone based on that relationship.

Everyone's emotional at this time, and their true feelings toward family members or the person who passed show themselves.

After the immediate shock and wailing, usually people start to prepare for the funeral arrangements and repast. Funerals are very expensive, and if this was not discussed beforehand with the person who passed, it can be very confusing as well. The main person responsible holds a lot of the weight in the decision-making, which brings on a lot of pressure. However, it also serves a healthy purpose and distraction for the moment.

My father's funeral was about two weeks after his passing so we could arrange everything. Because I am a part of a beautiful blended family, every side had to be considered—rightfully so.

It was interesting to observe because, like I said, family dynamics really come up to the surface at this time, and everyone has a different experience with the person who passed. Especially if the person who passed is older in age, imagine how many seasons of their lives were filled with different groups of people.

After all the planning, the beautiful celebration of life comes. My father's funeral was beautiful. I remember his job having a Metro bus outside since he worked for Metro, as an engineer, for 20-something years.

At the same time, I was ready for it to be done. I was tired of the calls, texts, and arrangements. I've always played peacemaker in my family, and I wanted my own peace.

The celebration of life is emotional, filled with tears, wailing, and memories of the loved one who passed. It is also a time we often hear a Word on making a decision to give your life to Christ and to also appreciate others while they are alive.

It usually ends with a legacy statement about how this person will be remembered through their family, friends, and the work they've done on earth. Of course, each celebration of life is unique to the person, but that tends to be the typical theme.

Then, the repast comes. Everyone is comforting, laughing, and illustrating a beautiful togetherness that quickly ends when everyone goes home.

Once everyone goes home, you go home too. If your loved one transitioned at home, you go back home to an empty house. My mother and I still lived at our family home because I promised my father that I would stay there for a while instead of leaving immediately (which he knew was my defense mechanism at the time—to leave).

After that day ends, the next day comes. Then the next. Then the next.

Then work calls.

Then school begins.

Then bills show up.

Then holidays approach.

Then people stop texting.

Then people stop calling.

Then life just continues on—yet you're still thinking about everything that occurred with your loved one passing.

As I said before, this is where grief begins. I like to describe grief as an inconvenience. It is quite rude because it comes up at the most inopportune time.

This is where you start to really feel the loss of that person. There is, sadly, no other way to fully appreciate someone in totality until they're gone. Until we experience life without a person, we will never fully understand what they brought to our life.

This is why we should be intentional, engaged, and appreciative while people are still here. But even with that intentionality, you will never know the full weight of someone's presence until it is no more.

Similar to me, I didn't know all that my father did for me until he was gone. My mother and I had to figure out a lot—and much of that was on her. As his spouse, his financial responsibilities became hers to manage among other things.

Not only that, but we had to learn how to be mother and daughter without my father. I was closer to my dad growing up, so this was a tough pill to swallow. Now, looking back, I am so grateful for my mother — but I'll get to that more later in this book.

The point is, when everyone else goes home and continues with their lives, you now have to embark on a new journey. A journey of living life without this person. A journey of living life while knowing what death caused in your family. A journey of living with the reality that tomorrow is never promised.

You now say those cliché phrases, "live like there's no tomorrow" and "cherish your loved ones," with experience, not just intelligence. It's easy to say those words, but now you're actually living them. Because for someone you cared deeply about, tomorrow didn't come.

But don't forget, God is greater, and He is omnipresent. He is there with you.

A New Beginning

While God is with you, you get to decide how to shape this new, unwanted journey. It will come with hard days and moments where the littlest thing can cause you to break down. All of that is normal.

It may also come with new supports, new perspectives, new dates to remember, and a new way to draw to God. But you get to choose.

Embarking on this new journey without God may feel easier at first, but it will get more burdensome along the way. All the things we've already discussed in this book are there to help you navigate grief with God, not without Him.

It hurts my heart to see people walk away from faith because of grief. And at the same time, I get it. Even though I did counseling, I shut God out for years. I didn't do what I am telling you to do.

Grief is already hard. Don't take the harder route. Take the new route that allows your burden to be cast, made light, and your yoke easy.

> *"For my yoke is easy, and my burden is light."* (Matthew 11:30)

> *"The Lord is near to the brokenhearted and saves those who are crushed in spirit."* (Psalm 34:18)

> *"He will never leave you nor forsake you."* (Deuteronomy 31:6)

In closing, remember you get to start a new path after this. Though what was no longer is, what can be still awaits you. New does not mean the absence of pain, it means the presence of God in the pain.

When no one else remembers the anniversary dates, birthdays, or death dates like you, God will. When your phone gets quiet and your home is vacant, God is there with you so you no longer have to feel alone.

This will be a new way to connect with God and it is a beautiful one.

Take a moment to acknowledge His presence right now and let that be a soothing comfort to you in times of isolation and despair.

To help, write down this affirmation as a reminder:

"God is with me and I am never alone. This may be the end of what was, and at the same time it is the beginning of something new. I choose to figure out this new journey with God."

Place it somewhere visible like a bathroom mirror to recite it daily. Your new beginning starts here.

DEVOTIONAL REFLECTION

READ:

Psalm 40:3 — *"He has given me a new song to sing, a hymn of praise to our God. Many will see what he has done and be amazed. They will put their trust in the LORD."*

REFLECT:

Take some time to reflect on this chapter. What new things have you implemented after losing your loved one? What old thoughts about grief do you need to let go of?

REMEMBER:

"New does not mean the absence of pain, it means the presence of God in the pain."

CHAPTER 8:
LAMENTING WELL

"I give you glory with my grief."

Have you ever read the Book of Lamentations? Though short, it is so impactful. It's poetic and records the tears of God's people, while also giving a future hope. The Prophet Jeremiah laments for God's people during their rebellion, destruction, God's just anger, and their return back to God through repentance.

In Chapter 3, we see Jeremiah turning from anguish to hope as he recalls God's faithfulness and acknowledges how they were not consumed due to the Lord's mercies.

> *"Because of the Lord's great love we are not consumed, for his compassions never fail. They are new every morning; great is your faithfulness."* (Lamentations 3:22–23)

Though God disciplined them like a good Father would, He remained faithful to restore them as Jeremiah pleaded with God to return them back to Him and renew their days (Lamentations 5:19-22).

Though it doesn't say it explicitly, I am sure people lost their lives during this time. Jeremiah was grieved because of the people's rebellion and he took his laments to God, acknowledged his human feelings, remembered that God is greater, and placed his hope in Him on behalf of the people.

We must remember that while we are lamenting, we have to reach that same turning point. We must remember that God's mercies won't allow us to be consumed because He loves us and His compassion never fails. They are new every single morning.

So What Does it Mean to Lament Well?

I remember telling a friend that grief isn't going anywhere, as she was battling out the initial pain of grief. It was hard to say this and I'm sure hard to hear, but I wish someone had told me that when I was at the beginning of my grief.

I wondered how long I would have random outbursts. How long I would need to anticipate the holiday season. How long I would be reminded of my loved ones through the littlest things. I wondered how long the guilt would feel when I did nice things for myself in February— the month that they passed.

The truth is and was, it would be here for a lifetime. As long as we live on this earth, there are things that we will have to deal with until we are on the other side of eternity.

But nothing is too hard for God to handle, over and over again.

Wailing, mourning, and crying are appropriate responses to grief. Mourning doesn't mean you lack faith. The fact that Lamentations was worthy enough to be a book means that God does not despise lamenting. **He responds to it.** He wants you to feel, cry, and have these moments — **but not to set up a tent there.**

In the previous chapter, I mentioned how the enemy can use your pain as a tool to keep you in bondage. He does not play fair and it's important to remember you have a real enemy out there, prowling to seek who he can devour.

When a memory would come back up in my mind, I'd have to make the choice on whether to sit with it for hours playing it over and over again in my mind, or to lament it well unto God.

Over time, I learned to **choose** the latter. That allowed space for both my emotions and for God to take it on. The Holy Spirit can help you overcome what you're feeling without making you a robot.

Here are a few things to help you lament well while placing your hope in God. Its been 12+ years later, and I still do this.

Let's start with the spiritual ways to lament well since the spiritual realm is far greater than the physical.

> *"For the things that are seen are transient, but the things that are unseen are eternal."* (2 Corinthians 4:18)

1. Put on Your Spiritual Armor.

There are 6 pieces of armor you will need. One of them is your **shield of faith** to block and destroy the fiery darts that come.

> *"In addition to all this, take up the shield of faith, with which you can extinguish all the flaming arrows of the evil one."* (Ephesians 6:16)

Your shield of faith is your belief and trust in God.

> *"You are my hiding place and my shield; I put my hope in Your Word."* (Psalm 119:114)

In order to be shielded, covered, and surrounded by God, you need to believe His Word. Without faith it is impossible to please God (Hebrews 11:6). You need to believe God is with you and your grief.

Secondly, your shield of faith is the Word of God because we gain faith by hearing.

> *"So then faith comes by hearing, and hearing by the word of God."* (Romans 10:17).

Start listening to sermons specific to grief, hope, peace, or love. Or use the message of a specific sermon to relate to your grief.

2. Guard Your Heart, Guard Your Gates.

"Above all else, guard your heart, for everything you do flows from it." (Proverbs 4:23)

You guard your heart by guarding your gates. Be careful who you listen to during this time or what songs are playing. Be mindful about what you watch. Be mindful about what you say out of your mouth and what others are saying too. Be wise about how much you share on social media.

Social media has its benefits, but remember what you put on the internet stays there. Ask yourself these questions:

- What message am I sending to others with this post?
- What does it say about where I am with my grief?
- Is this a safe space for my heart?
- What is my motive?

If the motive is validation, affirmation, or attention—you need to check your heart and guard it. Social media will not fill your voids.

For a while I could not hear the word cancer, nor could I watch a show that illustrated someone having it. For a while, I could not hear testimonies about people overcoming illnesses and how God did a miracle for them. For a while, my co-workers saw more patients who had a loss than I did. For a while, I did not look at babies without a heartache. It is okay to safeguard yourself as you recover and heal.

3. Listen to Praise & Worship Music or Make a Playlist.

You have to command your spirit to bless God in the midst of grief. Sometimes you'll feel like it and sometimes you won't— do it anyway.

> *"Praise the Lord, my soul; all my inmost being, praise his holy name."* (Psalm 103:1)

Worship causes all deceptive spirits to bow. Worship tunes out the noise in your head. Worship magnifies the Lord, making Him greater than your grief.

Here are a few songs I played:

- Speak to my Heart by Donnie McClurkin
- Be Healed by Canton Jones
- Flow to You by Bishop Paul S. Morton
- Holy Spirit by Jesus Culture
- No One Higher by Aaron Shust
- Here I am to Worship by Hillsong
- Surrounded by Bethel Music and Kari Jobe
- Mercy/Tremble by Housefires

Remember right after David lost his son, he worshipped God. (2 Samuel 12:20)

4. **Use Your Mouth to Create the Atmosphere You Want.**

Yes, you have the power to create with your mouth.

> *"Death and life are in the power of the tongue, and those who love it will eat its fruit."* (Proverbs 18:21)

Start speaking over your life. Start declaring your healing. Start speaking to yourself. In **Psalm 43**, you see the psalmist speaking to his/her self. **Verse 5** indicates the shift:

> *"Why, my soul, are you downcast? Why so disturbed within me? Put your hope in God, or I will yet praise him, my Savior and my God."* (Psalm 43:5)

Declare over yourself:

- I am healed.
- I am whole.
- This hard time does not define me.
- God is greater than my grief.
- I am restored.

Write them on a post it note and stick it on your mirror if you have to.

5. **Pray Persistently!**

> *"Rejoice always, **pray without ceasing**, give thanks in all circumstances; for this is the will of God in Christ Jesus for you."* (1 Thessalonians 5:17-18)

Pray through the sad memories. Pray for others who may be grieving too—because this takes your eyes off of you and onto God's people.

Pray for your other family members who are grieving along with you. **This is the will of God for you.**

And to dive deeper, here are a few things to pray through specifically:

- The holidays are a time when loss feels very heavy. It feels like something may be missing. Every year, it's like grief just knows the timing, and for me, I start feeling off around November up until February.

- I learned to pray in advance about these months. I prayed for togetherness, family time, love, peace, and comfort. I prayed that it would be months of remembering my losses with good memories and not isolating myself with the bad ones.

- I started to pray through sad memories. While it's important to reflect and let the emotions flow, it's also important to **renew and direct** your mind. This was the best thing I could do for myself. That allowed me to enjoy the holiday season the way I wanted to.

- **Pray over your heart and mind. May it be guarded with God's peace.** You may not feel like peace is permeating, but by faith, you can be assured that God's peace has and is keeping you.

   "And the peace of God, which transcends all understanding, will guard your hearts and your minds in Christ Jesus." (Philippians 4:7)

Grief has a messy way of allowing you to honor your loved one and, at times, holding you back. But with God in it, there is a way to move forward and a light to see in what can be a very dark space.

6. **Renew Your Mind in The Word.**

When your mind and emotions are in turmoil, take on the Sword of the Spirit which is the Word of God (Ephesians 6:17), which is sharper than any two-edged sword. The Sword of the Spirit will penetrate thoughts that try to haunt you.

Renewing your mind in His Word will keep you secure and stable. The first step may be hearing the Word, but you also need to meditate on the Word. That is how you go from information to transformation. That is how your mind is renewed.

> *"The Lord is close to the brokenhearted and saves those who are crushed in spirit."* (Psalm 34:18) which secured me in not being alone.

> *"Weeping may endure for a night, but joy comes in the morning."* (Psalm 30:5) which secured me in restoration.

> *"Blessed are those who mourn, for they will be comforted."* (Matthew 5:4) which secured me in comfort.

> *"For though we walk in the flesh, we do not war according to the flesh. For the weapons of our warfare are not carnal but mighty in God for pulling down strongholds, casting down arguments and every high thing that exalts itself against the knowledge of God, bringing every thought into captivity to the obedience of Christ"* (2 Corinthians 10:3-5) which secured me in spiritual warfare.

> *"For my thoughts are not your thoughts, neither are your ways my ways," declares the Lord. "As the heavens are higher than the earth, so are my ways higher than your ways and my thoughts than your thoughts."* (Isaiah 55:8-9) which secured me in God's sovereignty and ultimate plans.

Taking one day to "chew" on one scripture at a time will take up too much space for faulty beliefs to thrive. Each of these scriptures (plus many more) will keep you secure and illuminate how dark lamenting can feel, because the entrance of God's Word brings light. (Psalm 119:130)

7. **Rejoice and Give Thanks.**

> *"Rejoice always, pray without ceasing, **give thanks in all circumstances;** for this is the will of God in Christ Jesus for you."* (1 Thessalonians 5:17-18)

Sometimes learning to thank God while lamenting and suffering is the best medicine after all. Learn to give thanks to God because while doing so, you start to remember all that you should be thankful for.

While Jeremiah was lamenting, he still thanked God. While Paul suffered, he still rejoiced. While Job endured losses, he still kept the fear of the Lord.

Gratitude unto the Lord will allow you to look forward to what's ahead, not what is behind.

"I consider that our present sufferings are not worth comparing with the glory that will be revealed in us." (Romans 8:18)

Now, on the practical side of things—here are some things to do:

1. Read books.

I love books, and here are some good ones you can read to navigate your grief. It may not be specifically about grief, but it can help with your grief.

- Victorious Emotions by Wendy Backlund
- It's Not Supposed to Be This Way by Lisa TerKeust
- Wholeness by Toure Roberts
- My Words of Affirmation by Lisa Ann-Marie Stanford (wink)

2. Make Space to Honor Your Losses.

Before I expand, let me clarify that I do **not** mean meeting, speaking to, or manifesting your past loved one. **This is a Christian book, so I may not need to say that, but I did anyway.**

The Bible speaks against that and any type of divination:

"Let no one be found among you... who practices divination or sorcery, interprets omens, engages in witchcraft, or casts spells... or who consults the dead." (Deuteronomy 18:10-11)

You're **not** creating any altars for the dead here. What you are doing instead is remembering their life as it was before the pain came into play.

You are doing this for **you**, not to initiate some connection to them because they are no longer here. **Here are a few ideas:**

- You can enjoy their favorite restaurant or food.
- You can visit the cemetery. **Not** to meet them there, but as a formality.
- Journal a letter to release pent-up feelings.
- Watch their favorite show.
- Do something you shared.
- Make a photo album.
- Continue their business if applicable.
- Look at their pictures and cry.

These are just a few, but do what works for you. I got a bracelet with a dove on it and a "Z" to represent my father and baby. I don't wear it all the time, but I wear it on their death anniversaries. I often watch *Family Feud*, which was me and my dad's favorite show. I visit the cemetery when I feel led to.

On Mother's Day, I celebrate my journey and experience, and I also pour into the mothers in my life.

My mom and I got balloons for my dad's 10-year death anniversary and were able to grieve and celebrate together. I get to cook my dad's favorite foods such as curry goat and oxtail when my family & I cook for special occasions. And I shared my journey of grief on social media.

Disclaimer: Social media requires boundaries. During my earlier years of grief, I used social media as a punching bag. I was very vulnerable with the wrong crowd. I had to learn what to share on social media because social media is a place for much output with very little input. I was pouring out my tender heart and not receiving anything back. So, use wisdom with this. If you do not want something repeated or thrown back in your face to hurt you years down the line, do not put it on social media.

Everyone will come around you when you are healed and whole. But not everyone will be present when you are broken and hurt. **You don't owe everyone the details.** Save that for a safe support system.

All of the above things are coming out of a place of **honoring my experiences**, and it is okay if it looks different year to year. **You aren't practicing rituals.** You are making space to feel, reflect, express, and remember them in the best way possible.

3. **Share Your Grief with Others.**

Though they may not always understand, it's okay to say, "Hey, I'm feeling down today." My very close friends know February is a touchy month for me. It has gotten better over the years, but they still check in.

I stopped expecting them to always remember, even though it may hurt if they don't. But even if the check-in comes later on, it still counts. It is also my responsibility to share how I'm feeling.

Choose **safe people**, of course. You're not looking for quantity here. **You're looking for quality.**

4. Be Intentional With Your Time During the Holidays.

It's a busy time, which is good in a way, but you could also become overly busy, and that can trigger a breakdown. This is for anyone, but especially for someone grieving. Within your control, **pace yourself.**

Set days to do your Christmas shopping ahead of time. If people ask you to hang out, go hang out if your schedule allows. Do fun stuff with family, but do not overbook!

Grief makes it easy to say, *"Sorry, I can't make it."* But you can. Don't let grief stop you from living. Just bring it along with you.

Try to have at least one day to yourself, or maybe one morning or afternoon, to just **breathe**. The holidays already take up so much space, and they don't need to compete with your grief.

5. Create a Comforting Environment at Home or Outside.

Include self-care activities, solo dates, baked goods, candles, and time to rest. You need time to let your mind, body, and spirit rest. If you are married, be vocal with your partner about what you need. They are **not** mind readers.

Create a space where you can cry, pray, and still thrive. For me, I enjoy scheduling out solo dates to try new things like a cake decorating class, perfume making class, or pottery class. I also spend time at home in February so I can rest and indulge in some self-care.

Just because life moves on so fast doesn't mean you have to. Sometimes you need to be ministered to like Elijah when the angel gave him food to eat for his journey ahead (**1 Kings 19:5-7**), after he had been feeling so depleted and depressed.

Take this time to comfort yourself and I am sure the Lord will minister to you.

6. Surround yourself with Community and/or Ministry.

Don't overwhelm yourself with ministry, but be around the brethren.

This is not the time to stop going to church. This is actually the time to attend more and be around other uplifting people.

> *"Perfume and incense bring joy to the heart, and the pleasantness of a friend springs from their heartfelt advice."* (Proverbs 27:9)

Spend time with your community, your family and friends, especially when you may start to notice yourself pulling away. Isolation is very different from times of consecration or Godly solitude. Discern the difference and move accordingly.

7. Book That Counseling Appointment.

I am a little biased because of my own profession, but it is good to seek outside counsel. If you can get a Christian counselor, even better.

Grief is a journey, so there is no harm in having someone who can support you along the way especially when one or all of these above practical coping strategies fail.

You are allowed to talk to someone and you shouldn't feel guilty about that either. God places people in our lives to help us.

Sometimes, grief support groups are also helpful so you can hear other people's experiences and be strengthened in numbers than doing this all alone. My church has a grief share program and it has been such a blessing to many. Don't miss out on the support available to you. I really hope these are helpful for you!

Saying *"they are in a better place"* never worked for me personally, but these coping strategies have.

Remember: There is no script or right/wrong way to grieve. It never goes away; it only grows with you. There is **peace, comfort, acceptance, and love** on the other side to help you through the pain, sadness, and emptiness. God can fill you to the point where you are able to acknowledge what's been lost and still be full of what remains.

Lastly, you don't need to figure this all out now. Take in some of these coping skills and do one of them, then go back to reality. Be **proactive** about your grief instead of being reactive and you will learn what actually works along the way. God is with you.

DEVOTIONAL REFLECTION

READ:

Psalm 30:5 — "Weeping may endure for a night, but joy comes in the morning."

REFLECT:

Take some time to reflect on this chapter. What does lamenting well look like for you? How can you implement some of these strategies?

REMEMBER:

"God does not despise lamenting. He responds to it. He wants you to feel, cry, and have these moments — but not to set up a tent there."

CHAPTER 9:
YOUR NEW BEST FRIEND

"You're the greatest Teacher, You've counseled me."

It would be remiss not to mention someone who has been vital in my journey with grief, and as a Christian overall. This person has led me to the place I am at now and if you are looking for someone to buddy up with for your grief, I have the perfect person to help you along the way.

Let me introduce you to the **Holy Spirit**.

The Holy Spirit wasn't just introduced in Acts. He was mentioned as the Helper that would help us along our Christian journey when Jesus Christ was about to ascend. However, the Holy Spirit has been present since Genesis.

> *"Now the earth was formless and empty, darkness was over the surface of the deep, and the Spirit of God was hovering over the waters."* (Genesis 1:2)

We see here that the Spirit of God has been ever-present. In a dark, empty, and formless world, the Spirit of God was brooding over the waters.

We see the Spirit of God operating in the Old Testament, though He was specific to certain individuals and tasks. In **Judges 14:6**, it says:

> *"The Spirit of the Lord came powerfully upon him (Samson) so that he tore the lion apart with his bare hands as he might have torn a young goat."*

This is the same Spirit that was also prophesied to dwell in us in the New Testament. In **Ezekiel 36:27**, it says:

> *"And I will put my Spirit in you and move you to follow my decrees and be careful to keep my laws."*

And in **Joel 2:28** it says:

> *"And afterward, I will pour out my Spirit on all people. Your sons and daughters will prophesy, your old men will dream dreams, your young men will see visions."*

Then we see in the New Testament, **Acts 1:8**, Jesus tells His disciples:

> *"But you will receive power when the Holy Spirit comes on you; and you will be my witnesses in Jerusalem, and in all Judea and Samaria, and to the ends of the earth."*

And in **Acts 2:4**, it says:

> *"All of them were filled with the Holy Spirit and began to speak in other tongues as the Spirit enabled them."*

Again, we see that the same Spirit of God that was brooding over the earth is the same Spirit of God that has now entered His people and enabled them with tongues, power, and the ability to move with grace over their lives.

Then in **John 14:26**, Jesus teaches:

> *"But the Advocate, the Holy Spirit, whom the Father will send in my name, will teach you all things and will remind you of everything I have said to you."*

Just with these few texts, we see different characteristics of the Spirit of God, which, as we know, is God Himself.

We see **the Holy Spirit** being who He is, even in a formless world—having all power to create something out of nothing. We see Him giving us power, and now He is **within** us rather than **outside** of us. We see Him as an **Advocate**, an **Intercessor**, and a **Teacher** who will remind us of the Word of God, help us understand, and convict our spirits.

There is so much more to the Holy Spirit, but just looking at these texts makes me feel confident in trusting Him with anything.

He is the deep searcher who searches all things and knows the mind of God.

> *"The Spirit searches all things, even the deep things of God."* (1 Corinthians 2:10)

He is the **Spirit of Truth**, guiding us all to truth.

"But when he, the Spirit of truth, comes, he will guide you into all the truth." (John 16:13)

He is our Helper—and the Greek word for that is **Paraklētos** which means "one called to one's aid" which can be in the form of an advocate or comforter.

We would not be able to understand the things of God without the Spirit revealing it. There are areas of your grief that **only the Spirit of God can reveal**, so that you can be free. There are areas of your grief that **only the Spirit of God can comfort**, so that you can be restored. There are areas of your grief that **only the Spirit of God can help you with**, so that you can heal.

The Holy Spirit is necessary in your grief journey because He is able to turn a situation around that you would not be able to do on your own. He is able to restore what was lost and turn your grief into gratitude.

Now, how does He do this? In fellowship with Him. I've learned that the more **we fellowship with the Holy Spirit**, the better. He is a person and acknowledging Him as such is the first step.

The Holy Spirit has senses just like human beings do. He can see, hear, speak, and feel. One of the scriptures I reference is Ephesians 4:30 which says, *"And do not grieve the Holy Spirit of God, with whom you were sealed for the day of redemption."*

A force cannot be grieved, only a person can. Now, there are three ways to fellowship *with* The Holy Spirit that I'd like to share with you.

1. **The first way to fellowship is by speaking to Him.**

How do you know someone you do not speak to? How do you expect to be healed without reaching out?

The Holy Spirit already knows how you are feeling, but confessing it is letting Him have it so that you do not need to bear the burden alone.

> *"Cast all your anxiety on Him because He cares for you."* (1 Peter 5:7)

Casting your cares unto Him is for your benefit. It is not to cause shame or pain, it's for your freedom.

Because grief is layered and complex, it's important to have heart conversations with the Holy Spirit every step of the way. The Holy Spirit wants to deal with a **raw heart**, not one of stone. So sharing your feelings with Him is **necessary.**

The same way many people fellowship with friends, family, or their church community is similar to how you can fellowship with The Holy Spirit. The same way many people set calendar dates to hang out is the same way you can make time to hang out with Him and speak to Him.

One of the things I love and also try to be is an honest friend. As you speak and acknowledge The Holy Spirit, He will guide you into truth(as referenced earlier — **John 16:13**.

Once you are done speaking to Him, take time to listen. Listen out for that quiet, still voice that penetrates the heart. He doesn't just speak just to speak. He only speaks the truth.

One thing the Holy Spirit spoke to me about was my abandonment issues. I felt like my father gave up and left me to fend for myself while everyone else around me had both of their parents. Because of that abandonment, I didn't trust God either, thinking He would abandon me too.

Through this hard conversation, the truth set me free and after many years of not being able to call God "Father" (outside of prayer), "Abba", or "Daddy"... I can genuinely call Him that now. That came from honest conversations with The Holy Spirit which led to healing.

2. Another way to fellowship with Him is worship.

Spending time in worship is a beautiful way for the Holy Spirit to reveal things to you, because your focus isn't on yourself, but on God. In worship, He can gently reveal something you've been suppressing. Worship is the most sacred place for an exchange of your pain for His love.

It gives you a soft place to land. Because truthfully, some of the things we may feel while grieving are hard to accept, hard to share, and hard to recover from.

Spending time in His presence creates an atmosphere of comfort, of peace, and turns into a balm of healing so that you can be better than how you were before. God is committed to your transformation by revealing Himself to you. And you can do this while still honoring who you lost and remembering what you had with them.

Jesus lives in the duality of things. You can be grateful and grieving. He is the **Lion and the Lamb**, the **First and the Last**, the **Author and Finisher of your faith**. He is and will always be there on either side of the spectrum, so He can absolutely be there for your life and your loss.

Another outcome of worshipping is experiencing joy. In His presence, there is fullness of joy (Psalm 16:11).

Worship makes grief very small compared to the great God we serve. I have been able to find so much joy after spending time with The Holy Spirit. I start to forget about all my worries and leave lighter than before. There's an exchange that occurs that is unexplainable.

> *"To console those who mourn in Zion, To give them beauty for ashes, The oil of joy for mourning, The garment of praise for the spirit of heaviness; That they may be called trees of righteousness, The planting of the Lord, that He may be glorified."* (Isaiah 61:3)

3. The third way to fellowship with Him is intercession.

Intercession is prayer that involves going to someone to make a plea — or to entreat, ask someone earnestly. In the Bible we see countless examples of intercession.

Abraham intercedes for Sodom which led to the rescue of Lot (Genesis 18 and 19).

In Daniel 9, he turns his face to the Lord seeking and pleading for mercy on behalf of the people.

In Acts 7, Stephen pleads that God forgives his executioners.

On the Cross, Jesus intercedes for his tormentors, showing compassion and mercy in the midst of suffering and taking on the world's transgressions (Luke 23:34).

Lastly, The Holy Spirit intercedes or advocates on our behalf.

"In the same way, the Spirit helps us in our weakness. We do not know what we ought to pray for, but the Spirit himself intercedes for us through wordless groans. And he who searches our hearts knows the mind of the Spirit, because the Spirit intercedes for God's people in accordance with the will of God." (Romans 8:26-27)

When we are left in uncertainty, the Spirit of God intercedes for us. We may not know what else to say or how to explain how we feel. But the Spirit of God knows what to pray for and will conform us into Jesus. There are bigger things to pray for **beyond your grief**.

I remember praying one night and out of nowhere, I started to pray for my mother. I always pray for my mother but this time was different.

I started to pray for her healing and restoration. Then I was led to praying over my womb and childbirth. Then I was led to praying over my kids. Then I was led to pray over my daughter's wombs. And I kept going and going. What started off as prayer for me, led to prayer for those attached to me (and I don't have any living kids yet).

When we are allowing the Spirit of God to intercede through us, **He leads us** into prayers we never even thought about. He goes deep in our past, far in our future, while staying present with us. He covers the things we can't due to our human limitations.

My healing wasn't just about me, **it was about my lineage.** In fact, this is why I am writing this book.

This book would have been about my pain if written years ago, but 12+ years later, it is written about God's purpose.

This is why God is greater than grief. Because grief will keep you focused on what is happening. Meanwhile, God is focused on where you are going and as we use our grief for His glory, **we'll see nothing is of waste.**

It brings comfort knowing that The Holy Spirit is speaking to God on our behalf, as our advocate. It brings comfort knowing that when we feel weak, the Holy Spirit is communicating for us. It brings comfort knowing that The Holy Spirit is praying in alignment with God's perfect will.

This is why intercession is important. We are literally in fellowship with Him as He prays for us and through us with wordless groanings that are deeper than what we can say.

> *"But you, beloved, building yourselves up on your most holy faith, praying in the Holy Spirit..."* (Jude 1:20)

Intercede in your spiritual tongue often because it builds up your spiritual life and aforementioned, you will be speaking mysteries and prayers that go beyond you and your grief.

In closing, the thing about all of these modes of fellowship is that you can easily mimic these with other things or people. That is a slippery slope. God created us intentionally desiring **community, advocacy, and worship.**

We often spend time in endless conversations with our friends or family (speaking). We devote our hearts, time, money, and energy to things to receive peace, joy, and love (worship). And we thrive off of feeling validated, secure, and protected by people (advocacy).

And while all of these things have its benefits, it can become a problem when they become our source.

Healing often becomes complicated when we seek idols to heal us.

We go to people, work, ministry, money, or other things and expect them to save us. And even though it may be a good thing, that doesn't mean it can't become an idol.

"You shall have no other gods before me." (Exodus 20:3)

Healing takes time. And since we live in a world where instant gratification is a thing, I understand the impatience and discomfort that may come as you sit with your grief.

Anyone would want to quickly fix it, but be careful not to allow these things to take **precedence over God Himself**.

In **Exodus 15:26**, the Lord reveals Himself:

"I am the LORD, who heals you."

There's nothing He can't heal you from and He doesn't need help.

Go to God first. Let The Holy Spirit be your best friend. He wants to fellowship with you and heal your grief.

DEVOTIONAL REFLECTION

READ:

1 Corinthians 2:10 – "The Spirit searches all things, even the deep things of God."

REFLECT:

Take some time to reflect on this chapter. How do you plan to fellowship with the Holy Spirit more than before?

REMEMBER:

"When we are left in uncertainty, the Spirit of God intercedes for us. We may not know what else to say or how to explain how we feel. But the Spirit of God knows what to pray for."

CHAPTER 10:
THAT HEALETH THEE...

"Okay, God, I see what you're doing now."

Healing has become this generation's favorite thing to do and talk about, as well as **self-care**. There is a difference between how we heal as believers and how we heal in the world. There are practical things to do, such as self-help books, **Christian-based** books, podcasts, journaling, and therapy—many of these things are what I mentioned in the previous chapter.

While I believe in these things, **I believe in Jesus more**.

I have come from therapy and books still feeling empty and vacant. That made it clear that there are some places that only God can reach. It makes me think of the woman with the issue of blood in Luke 8.

She struggled with this blood issue for 12 years, and I am sure she did not sit and wait until she heard Jesus was coming to find her healing. I am sure she went to doctors, tried medicine, read books, and did practical things to heal herself or cope with her disease. Yet, when she heard Jesus was coming, she stood on her faith alone.

She didn't ask to make an appointment, have a healing ceremony, or demand He touch her. She took it upon herself and said…

*"If I only touch His cloak, I will be healed." (*Matthew 9:21)

She took ownership of her healing and took it by force. This not only indicates boldness, faith, and courage, but also humility.

There are many people who have prayed for healing and have not received it just yet, but they still believe. They are still holding on, and they are still having faith that Jesus is the Lord who heals. Similarly, she did not approach this with an obligation to be healed—she did it out of pure faith.

Sometimes, practical things may not help right away. It will not be enough, just like it wasn't enough for me. **You need that touch from the hem of His garment.**

All you need is Jesus to just walk by with your hand stretched out.

Jesus felt the power that left Him and said, *"Daughter, your faith has healed you. Go in peace and be freed from your suffering."* (Mark 5:34)

Because grief is such a long-term situation, it is imperative to always have your hand stretched out for His garment. Because grief has a funny way of revisiting and making you feel like it's day one of grief again, it is imperative to go in peace and be freed.

This is something that you own and hold onto.

So, keep your faith and remind yourself that healing is your portion. It has already been settled on the Cross — even if it doesn't feel that way here on earth. **Jesus is more than enough to heal your disease.**

Now, you may be asking, *"How do you know you are healing?"* Well, let's talk through the phases.

The Broken Phase:

During this phase, your perspective is negative, hurtful, and painful. You may feel abandoned, confused, and bitter. This is a sensitive and vulnerable place. But the Holy Spirit meets you here, because He is near to the brokenhearted.

> *"The LORD is close to the brokenhearted and saves those who are crushed in spirit."* (Psalm 34:18)

The Bandage Phase:

This is the **pivotal choice point**. Will the world cover your wound, or will you let Jesus do it? Will you allow God into your pain?

This phase determines the direction of your healing. Some people self-medicate here. Some people turn away from the faith. Some people lose all hope. What are you going to do?

I hope your answer is: **Let God bandage you up.** And He does it with:

- **His Word**
- **His Presence**
- **His Community**

You need **all of the above**.

The Beautiful Phase:

This is when healing becomes glorious. You feel more whole. You start to see death differently. You recognize that God did not abandon you in your pain, He walked you through it. This is reflective of acceptance.

Let's break this down with real life examples.

Phase 1: Broken

During this phase of my life, I was angry and hurt, and I lacked accountability and discipleship.

Once I moved out of my parents' home I started wilding out. I started partying, having sex, and drinking more than I ever had in my life.

I vividly remember one night in grad school, I met up with a new friend who had just started the program too. We went out, and I had mixed light and dark liquor—which apparently is a big no-go. I wouldn't have known that because I had never drunk like that before, but I wanted to fit in. Out of my brokenness, I wanted to do whatever I wanted.

I ended up getting so drunk and vomiting a lot that night. I had to sleep over at this new friend's home, and that's how we bonded. From there, I increased my liquor tolerance so I could "hang" and hold my weight. I started to entertain any man and sleep around. I leaned even more on my feelings and neglected healing.

Eventually, I stepped down from ministry because my other life was becoming more important. Honestly, I didn't want to feel convicted anymore. Instead of repenting, I removed myself.

This was a broken place in my life. And most of the connections I made during this phase have now phased out too. Looking back, I really could have lost myself entirely.

Nothing good comes out of brokenness if you decide to stay there. Trying to fit in while broken is impossible— you won't fit anywhere. It became a comfortable distraction for me. It was a dirty bandage I didn't want to change.

Unbeknownst to me, this caused more infection. More feelings of abandonment surfaced when all these guys I was sleeping with didn't want me. This deepened the wound of what I lost, and I started to project that onto God.

The truth is, I was the one who left.

This phase resulted in bad decisions which allowed the enemy to make me believe nothing good could come from my life and that God had forgotten about me. It was a dark, dark place.

This phase is very vulnerable, and it's important to guard it the right way. Unfortunately, that was not my case—but thank God for **His grace and mercy.**

Phase 2: Bandage

Over time, the broken version of me became less satisfying. Everything I was doing seemed inadequate. Nothing was completing me.

I remember I was dating this guy, and we broke up in 2017. I remember to this day, crying in my living room and saying,

"God, I give you my relationships. I want something You have for me."

I believed that a relationship would fill the voids, so this was always my focus in prayer. After that, I lie to you not, every relationship I tried to entertain during this period did not work out and did not bear any good fruit. I started to feel convicted and numb at the same time. I started to feel the pain of my losses creeping back up to the surface.

During this time in my life, I was really depressed, angry, and not a healthy person. During the bandage period, it's hard to show up well. I tried to, but I was actively being wrapped up. And you know, wrapping up an infected, dirty, bleeding, oozing wound is going to hurt. You become needy, co-dependent, and start to affect others around you.

After living so far away for two years, I moved closer to my family and rented a room in someone's home to save money. I was closer to church, so I started to attend more regularly. I started to allow God to bandage me up, but little did I know, I would also have to **let go of the old bandages too.**

Phase 3: Beautiful

Now, this part didn't start off **beautiful**, but it ended that way.

As I mentioned in Chapter 3, by spring 2021, I had moved to my condo, and this is when my life changed. God confronted me. Honestly, this experience was divine. I was pretty much at a crossroads, and God was straight up. He asked me, "Is this what you want for the rest of your life?"

After confronting a lot of pain, most of which was associated with grief and my negative view of God, I decided to say **yes to His will, for real**.

After this, God took me on a journey:

- A journey of affirming me **in His Word** this time.
- A journey of real healing no therapist could take me through.
- A journey of heart surgery with stitches that wouldn't come undone.
- A journey of redefining myself without needing a man or a certain status.
- A journey of rediscovering me and my purpose.
- A journey of health and wellness; inside and out.

And through that, **He changed my story**. Through that, He began to change my poor characteristics in me with **gentleness**. Through that, **He restored** other relationships too.

Because grief is so multifaceted and shows up in all kinds of ways, He had to remake every single part of my life. He restored relationships that were broken—including family.

The restoration in my mother and I's relationship is one I am grateful for.

In the absence of my father, her and I have become a lot closer over the years. She has been on her own healing journey too—I can't imagine losing a spouse. In hindsight, I realize I am actually living out my mother's old prayers. Regardless of how estranged we were when I was in my broken and bandaged phases, she kept me covered in prayer. And our relationship is **beautiful** now.

I am grateful for how God restored me and my sister, my cousins, and my siblings on my dad's side. No one's family is perfect but it is far better than where it was. At the beginning, I said loss can bring a family together or tear a family apart. Glory to God, He has brought us back together in the **fullness of time.**

Most of these issues don't directly relate to grief and loss, but the grief and loss made them worse. So when God heals you, He isn't spot-treating your grief—He is healing all of you, and it will be beautiful.

Now, years later, I am whole. I have a great relationship with my family on both sides. I am active in ministry at church. I have healthy friendships and two businesses, and I pour into myself. I have found contentment in Christ, and through that, grief has dwindled. I reflect on way more good memories than bad memories now. And I look forward to having kids again one day; something I lost hope in.

"Indeed, God has turned my sorrow into joy." (Psalm 30:11)

So as you heal, you will change. The person you were before no longer exists—and that's okay. Healing has a way of deepening your relationship with God and redefining you. Or should I say, refining you.

Over time, as you heal, you will develop better, healthier expectations of people. As I've mentioned earlier in this book, not everyone will remember the date. Not everyone will be sensitive to the time you lost your loved one. Not everyone will understand how touchy holidays, birthdays, and life events are.

It's important that as you heal, your **expectations heal too**.

I used to get upset when I didn't get the type of support I needed. But I later had to realize that it is no one's responsibility but my own. Instead of looking to their support as the bandage, **I looked to Jesus**.

Now, that doesn't mean you don't reach out to others. There were times I had to reach out and be vulnerable and honest. When you need support, **do not hesitate**. That's part of the healing process.

You learn when and how to ask for support in a healthy way. **Community is very important**. The goal is not to depend on it.

Some healthy expectations to consider are:
- Expect friends to reach out in the way that they can.
- Support comes in different shapes and sizes
- Identify one person you can talk to—perhaps someone who has dealt with grief too
- Ask for prayer when you need it. You don't always have to go into detail but ask the brethren to cover

you in prayer while actively grieving (usually around the month the person died)
- Everyone won't remember and that is appropriate. Share a picture or fond memory instead — this invites them to remember and support you
- Some people are not comfortable talking about grief — pick up on the cues and find people who are
- It's healthy to take some appropriate space if necessary — perhaps letting your community know you need a week to yourself will suffice.
- The death anniversary date of your late loved one is just another day to someone else — don't take offense.

Every year will be different. It doesn't mean you are healing any more or any less. I finally got to a place where I didn't even post it on social media and I felt fine. I no longer **depended** on people's sympathies.

This is the beautiful phase.

Grief Into Gratitude:

Before we close this chapter, I want to touch on what I mean by gratitude.

Grief turns into **spiritual gratitude** when you start to focus on what your loved one in Christ has now. I got to the place where my father's healing was on the other side of eternity, and for that, I am grateful.

After all, eternity is what we should all look forward to. That stings, I know! But to be honest, that was the best way for me to cope. If I kept wondering why my father was not here on earth, it would cause me to regress.

Understanding will come later. There is a line between what we will understand here on earth and what we will understand in heaven (see *1 Corinthians 13:12*).

My father's and son's deaths have turned into a **lifetime purpose** for me. I wouldn't be writing this book or be passionate about motherhood if it weren't for them. I'd hoped it was under different circumstances, but God has a way of bringing things full circle.

He gives you a new song. (Psalm 40:3)

That exchange is painful and raw as you remove the old and bring in the new.

But soon, and very soon, you will adopt a new perspective, a new lens, a new story, a new heart, and **a new gratitude for life.** I do not take life for granted because I saw it slip away from two people I held close to my heart. That kind of gratitude only comes with experience.

You start thanking God differently. You start rejoicing differently when you come out of the ashes.

Healing is now your new, beautiful song.

Here are some gratitude prompts to reflect on:

I am grateful that life does not end on earth, but in eternity with Jesus Christ.

I am grateful for the support system I have around me.

I am grateful for the time I had with my loved one.

I am grateful for my healing and how God turned my pain into purpose.

I am grateful for restored relationships.

I am grateful for being able to use my story to encourage others.

I am grateful for the healing my loved one found on the other side.

I pray as you heal, you see the areas you left unattended too. I pray you come out of this whole, full, renewed, and healed in such a way that no one could even tell what you've been through.

What do they say again? You see the glory, but you don't know my story.

May your story reflect God's glory.

DEVOTIONAL REFLECTION

READ:

Matthew 9:21 — *"If I only touch His cloak, I will be healed."*

REFLECT:

Take some time to reflect on these 3 phases. Which phase are you at? How do you plan to move forward to the next stage? Also, identify one person you feel safe with to share your grief with when appropriate. How do you need support from them? Ask God for guidance.

REMEMBER:

"So when God heals you, He isn't spot-treating your grief — He is healing all of you, and it will be beautiful."

PART III:
BE READY

CHAPTER 11:
THE GATES OF HEAVEN

"I just wish you were still here."

The beautiful thing that occurs when someone we love dies is the hope of their **heaven-stamped** visa. You have hope as a believer to know that if your loved one was a believer, their place in eternity is sealed and secured.

"The Gates of Heaven" is the name of the cemetery where my father was buried. I always loved that name. There is a different sense of peace we have when we know that is where they ended up.

Let's look at what the Word tells us:

> *"Then I saw "a new heaven and a new earth," for the first heaven and the first earth had passed away, and there was no longer any sea. I saw the Holy City, the new Jerusalem, coming down out of heaven from God,*

prepared as a bride beautifully dressed for her husband. And I heard a loud voice from the throne saying, "Look! God's dwelling place is now among the people, and he will dwell with them. They will be his people, and God himself will be with them and be their God. He will wipe every tear from their eyes. There will be no more death or mourning or crying or pain, for the old order of things has passed away." He who was seated on the throne said, "I am making everything new!" Then he said, "Write this down, for these words are trustworthy and true." He said to me, "It is done. I am the Alpha and the Omega, the Beginning and the End. To the thirsty I will give water without cost from the spring of the water of life. Those who are victorious will inherit all this, and I will be their God, and they will be my children. But the cowardly, the unbelieving, the vile, the murderers, the sexually immoral, those who practice magic arts, the idolaters, and all liars, they will be consigned to the fiery lake of burning sulfur. This is the second death." (Revelation 21:1–8 NIV)

Thank God for His Word. He says there will be a new earth and heaven. **Behold, He makes all things new.** There will be no pain, tears, mourning, or sorrow. All things will have passed away, and everything will be made anew.

Isn't this something to look forward to? May this comfort you, to know that we all, as believers, have a beautiful, new heaven to look forward to. Some will get there sooner than others, but this is the assurance of our destination. If you read further in chapter 21, it describes **New Jerusalem** with gates and walls of jasper, crystal, and all kinds of rare jewels.

We will no longer need light or sun because God Himself will be our light (Revelation 22), and we will worship Him forever. This was always the plan, for God to be one with His people. **What a beautiful end to a destructive world.**

This is God's promise. And I know most people don't like to read Revelation, but this is where you get your faith for what's to come. Just knowing Jesus Christ is coming back is not enough. You need to know about His return and what will happen when He does return.

Add to your faith by knowing this, receiving this promise, and remembering that your loved one has this promise too. Even though they are gone from this earth, they still have this promise if they are in Christ.

Not only that, we will also receive new bodies. I know for me, it was hard to see my father slowly shrink away as time went on. It was hard to see him not look like himself at the funeral. And it's hard for most people to see their loved one when they are passing or have already passed.

For some, it is a process. For others, it is sudden. Either way, it is difficult to accept. That's why it's important to ask God to renew your mind daily.

I know for me, the painful images kept popping up in my mind, and the Lord delivered me from that. Like I mentioned before, it's okay to remember your loved one—but be mindful of the sorrowful memories, the ones that cause you to sink back into a dark place.

Let the Word of God remind you that their bodies will be made new. Ours will too. I know some of us have joked, *"So does that mean this weight will be gone too?"* (Ha!) It's not quite like that, but the point is there will be no more body aches, physical pain, or illness. **Our bodies will be glorified.** Made for heaven.

Let's look at Scripture on our heavenly bodies:

> *"For we know that when this earthly tent we live in is taken down (that is, when we die and leave this earthly body), we will have a house in heaven, an eternal body made for us by God himself and not by human hands. We grow weary in our present bodies, and we long to put on our heavenly bodies like new clothing. For we will put on heavenly bodies; we will not be spirits without bodies."* (1 Corinthians 15:35–38)

> *"While we live in these earthly bodies, we groan and sigh... but we want to put on our new bodies so that these dying bodies will be swallowed up by life. God himself has prepared us for this, and as a guarantee, He has given us His Holy Spirit."* (2 Corinthians 5:1–5 NLT)

The same way Jesus's body was bruised, torn, and abused so that we could be whole, **we too will be made anew.** His sacrifice wasn't just for us to enjoy life on earth free from sin. It was so we could live with assurance of life in heaven.

Losing a loved one, seeing their body decompose, and seeing their face change in the final moments is painful. But imagine the beauty of **your spirit being captured by God.** That very moment, He is there.

Think about those people who say they heard an airplane or saw a vision at the time of death. Even in that moment, God is **welcoming** them.

Reflect on Elijah's glorious departure with chariots of fire (2 Kings 2:11). Though that won't be everyone's experience, it assures me that **there is glory to behold** when one takes their last breath on earth.

When Jesus died, God was there. He committed His Spirit into His Father's hands — right there on the Cross (Luke 23:46). After your loved one died, **God was there too.** Their spirit is with Him until they (we) get our new glorified bodies.

And while you're grieving, **God is there.**

He is present at birth, present at death, and present in everything in between. He is God.

> *"Where can I go from your Spirit? Where can I flee from your presence? If I go up to the heavens, you are there; if I make my bed in the depths, you are there."*
> (Psalm 139:7-8 NIV)

There's no dominion, no realm, no stage of life or death He doesn't have access to. Let that be our solace. Let that be our assurance.

Let us begin to see some beauty in death for the believer. Let us look forward to what's ahead of us — and what some of our loved ones got to see earlier.

> *"For to me, to live is Christ, and to die is gain."*
> (Philippians 1:21 NIV)

> *"But in keeping with his promise, we are looking forward to a new heaven and a new earth, where righteousness dwells."* (2 Peter 3:13 NIV)

Now I know this may not make you feel better right away. The famous phrase, "They're in a better place," never worked for me either. But that's because my faith wasn't there yet.

I didn't know or see death this way, even as a believer. I always knew I'd go to heaven, but the revelation of what that citizenship meant was missing.

But I came to realize something: **this promise isn't based on your feelings—it's based on faith.**

You will still mourn. You will still grieve. You will still miss them. Even when you fully accept their death, it doesn't mean you approved of it.

But these scriptures give us hope, promise, and truth. And that truth is needed when the swarming thoughts try to take over your mind.

Everything is better **on the other side of eternity.** And we all will prayerfully get there one day.

The Gates of Heaven are **the entrance to eternity.** And that is something we should all look forward to.

> *"And He said to him, "Most assuredly, I say to you, hereafter you shall see heaven open, and the angels of God ascending and descending upon the Son of Man."* (John 1:51)

The Inevitable:

And in order to get there, we will either die by the grave or be caught up in the rapture with our Lord and Savior, after the Great Tribulation. Death is inevitable and it's important we remember that oftentimes, we fear death because we feel like we will be missing out. We are afraid of missing the people, the things, and not being able to see life all the way through. But as believers, we have this assurance to keep us grounded.

To live is for Christ, and when our days are fulfilled by His grace, we will gain a new life, a new body, and a new mind in Him. He will glorify our bodies into His (Philippians 3:21). There will be no more sin, sadness, tears, mourning, or the weight of grief (Revelation 21:4). What a joy to look forward to. Death is simply not the end. **It is the beginning of eternal life.**

Our suffering will yield joy. If you don't receive this truth, the circumstances of the world will consume you. It will crush you, and you won't have the spiritual strength to endure it. You need an anchor, and the Word of God is that anchor. God is greater!

However, until that time comes, **we have work to do on this earth.** It is difficult to keep going and pressing forward after losing someone you love. It can stop you in your tracks and cause you to question everything. Life becomes different after loss—figuring out how to proceed, how to balance, and how to move on without guilt becomes a journey of its own. It changes your routine. It changes how you think and feel. It changes you.

Personally, I've chosen not to take life for granted. I saw my father go from being this active, social, warm man to someone who could barely speak. His life began to decline the moment he was diagnosed with cancer, not just at the moment of death. I saw how his interests faded long before his final days. He didn't start losing his life at the time of death; it started long before.

It changed everything in our family drastically. From that moment on, I could never view life the same. I could never take for granted making it home after a grocery run, celebrating another birthday, seeing another year, or even getting normal results on a physical exam. You just never know. **While we believe and have faith that God is our keeper, we must also remember we are not here for long.**

We can't cling to this world more than we cling to Heaven, our true home and citizenship (Philippians 3:20). So, in the meantime, do not take life on earth for granted. When it's done, it's done. You will never get time back.

God created time and appointed times and seasons for each of us to fulfill His purposes on earth. Let us never take that for granted. May we be able to say, like Paul, that we ran our race and fulfilled it, no regrets, no purposes left undone (2 Timothy 4:7).

So, live purposefully now! Your loved one would want you to. The moment I stopped feeling guilty for living was a moment of liberation. My father would want that for me. He wouldn't want me stuck in my grief, paralyzed by the emotions, or held back by "what ifs." He would want me to feel and process my emotions well and also get up and seize the day.

This season of your life will not be wasted. God can use it for your good—for your purpose. These same purposes were predestined long ago.

> *"For we are his workmanship, created in Christ Jesus for good works, which God prepared beforehand, that we should walk in them."* (Ephesians 2:10)

Prepare for the day you might see Jesus. No one knows when that day will come, but it is our responsibility to prepare. Each day you wake up, you wake up with purpose. And each of us will give account for what we did according to God's will for our lives (see Romans 14:12).

Many people create wills and make arrangements so their children are cared for—which is important and responsible. But what about the **will of God** over your life? What are you doing with that? How are you stewarding this body and life to fulfill what God has called you to do?

We go to funerals and hear how the person impacted lives and left a legacy. **What will you be leaving behind?** Maybe the people impacted won't be your children, but someone may need what you created, produced, wrote, or shared so they can receive what God intended through you.

How will you use the pain of grief as motivation to fulfill your purpose?

God never promised a life without pain or trials. In fact, He said to *"take heart because He has already overcome the world"* (John 16:33). He teaches us how to suffer well and still press toward the mark (Philippians 3:14). Grief is just **one** of the sad circumstances we will face.

There is such a thing as **redemptive suffering**, where God allows certain trials that produce character, intimacy with the Lord, and purification. While He doesn't cause bad things to happen, He can use these experiences to bring to the surface the very things God wants to transform within us. That kind of **purposeful suffering** can lead you to serve others in ways you never expected.

In the midst of Joseph's suffering, he found favor with God and man (Genesis 39). God used his suffering as part of the restoration he experienced with his brothers he later forgave. I am sure Joseph's heart went through deep transformation, endurance, and character changes to yield such results.

> *"Not only that, but we rejoice in our sufferings, knowing that suffering produces endurance, and endurance produces character, and character produces hope."* (Romans 5:3-4)

When we shift our focus off ourselves and remember that we are in this world but not of it (**John 17:16**), we gain a better understanding and acceptance that all of this is temporary — a momentary life leading to an eternal reward.

After all He has gone to prepare the place for us, with many mansions to behold.

> *"I go to prepare a place for you. And if I go and prepare a place for you, I will come again and receive you to*

Myself; that where I am, there you may be also." (John 14:3)

And when you are face-to-face with Jesus Christ, **what will He say about you?** What will He say about how you served His kingdom? And if you go home to be with the Lord before His return, what will people say about the legacy you left behind?

The psalmist wrote something that has stayed with me:

"We will not hide them from their descendants; we will tell the next generation the praiseworthy deeds of the Lord, His power, and the wonders He has done." (Psalm 78:4)

Let that be our posture. I hope that whatever you do now can be told to the next generation.

Just like Joshua left behind memorial stones for the descendants of Israel to ask about God's mighty works (Joshua 4:6-7), you can leave "memorials", too. Let your life leave behind a trail of God's faithfulness. May the generations to come ask, **"Who was this person, and what did God do through them?"**

Let us go into all the world and preach the gospel, just as Jesus commissioned us to do (Mark 16:15). Let us not take life lightly anymore—because tomorrow is not promised (James 4:14). Let us not take it lightly—because we don't know the hour of Christ's return (Matthew 24:36). Let us not take life lightly—because we have Kingdom work to do. Let us not take life lightly—and have our oil ready like the wise virgins (Matthew 25:10).

When all is said and done, may it be said of us: A legacy was built, good works were left behind, and the future hope was not cut off (Proverbs 23:18).

Now, I know this was heavy. No one likes to dwell on the topic of death. Even writing this book was difficult for me. I had to think about death often—and thank God the Holy Spirit gave me the words and strengthened me as I wrote this.

To focus on grief without acknowledging death would be avoidance. **Grief is a result of death.** We can predict our birth date thanks to God's wisdom He gives doctors and due dates—but we cannot predict our death date. And we cannot predict the death dates of our loved ones either.

So don't let the enemy whisper lies to you. Set your mind on things above— spiritual and heavenly affairs (Colossians 3:2). Put your hope in the promise that God has given us a **full life span** in Jesus's name (Exodus 23:26) and satisfy me and you with long life (Psalm 91:16). Do not fear death for the Lord did not give us a spirit of fear, but of love, power, and a sound mind (2 Timothy 1:7).

And until He returns, **there is work to do.**

Let that work begin now with you going deeper with God and discovering your God ordained purpose. **Use your words to reshape your reality— with much prayer.** Use the **Word of God** to reframe your thinking (Romans 12:2). **Use prayer to guide your decisions.** Trust in Him, lean not on your own understanding, and He will direct your path **(Proverbs 3:5-6).**

He knows the plans He has for you (Jeremiah 29:11). And I pray you will continue your journey and complete the good work God began in you (Philippians 1:6) through Christ Jesus.

Death is inevitable. Live purposefully **now.**

DEVOTIONAL REFLECTION

READ:

Revelation 21:21-23 — *"The twelve gates were twelve pearls, each gate made of a single pearl. The great street of the city was of gold, as pure as transparent glass. I did not see a temple in the city, because the Lord God Almighty and the Lamb are its temple. The city does not need the sun or the moon to shine on it, for the glory of God gives it light, and the Lamb is its lamp."*

REFLECT:

Take some time to reflect on this chapter. How are you living purposefully now? What is God's purpose for your life? If you do not know, this is your time to find out and start.

REMEMBER:

"When we shift our focus off ourselves and remember that we are in this world but not of it (John 17:16), we gain a better understanding and acceptance that all of this is temporary — a momentary life leading to an eternal reward.

"And until He returns, there is work to do."

CHAPTER 12:
TWO DESTINATIONS, ONE HOPE

"He's in the best hands, the Father's hands."

As we end, I'd love to expand on the two destinations we all face before we accept Jesus Christ as our personal Lord and Savior. In the twinkling of an eye, the Lord may come and take those who belong to Him (1 Corinthians 15:52, Matthew 24:44). And I want you to search your heart and ask yourself: Am I sure that would be me?

If there's even an inkling of doubt, let's not even play with that. **Let's re-dedicate your life today.**

Heaven and Hell are two destinations for a person's eternal home (Revelation 21 and Revelation 14:11).

We will all have a passport, death or rapture will be the passport, **but what will be written on the documents?** How do you know you will be able to enter the Kingdom of God? How can you be 100% sure?

Here's how:

> *"If you declare with your mouth, 'Jesus is Lord,' and believe in your heart that God raised Him from the dead, you will be saved."* (Romans 10:9)

Accept Jesus Christ as your personal Lord & Savior today! There is no need to wait or think about this, especially in the times we are living in. The end is near, and while many have said that over the decades, there are present things happening that are clearly mentioned in the Word. Jesus tells us to **watch for the signs** so that we know when the end is approaching (Matthew 24:6-14).

So this isn't a cute thing to say to catch your attention. **It's the truth.**

You do **not** need to fear death as a believer. You do **not** need to fear the end times or rapture as a believer. This is where the enemy loves to paralyze believers. But trust and know that death or rapture is your passport to heaven.

We have no idea which one will come first, but we do know that God will fulfill the number of our days — the days ordained before they came to be (Job 14:5, Psalm 139:16). Jesus Christ has **defeated death**, and that is where we should place our hope, our faith, and our destination.

On earth, it is painful to lose someone; in our flesh, it hurts. But in our spirit, if we know that person was a believer, we rejoice.

> *"Then I heard a voice from heaven say, 'Write this: Blessed are the dead who die in the Lord from now on.' 'Yes,' says the Spirit, 'they will rest from their labor, for their deeds will follow them.'"* (Revelation 14:13)

As it says in Revelation, *blessed are the dead in the Lord.* There is nothing to fear there. Your eternal destination has been sealed.

> *"To live is for Christ, and to die is to gain."* (Philippians 1:21)

Your life is not cut off when your earthly body goes away or when you are **swept away** in the clouds. You live again with a new, glorified body, which Christ gave you (Philippians 3:21).

May every seed of fear that the devil has planted in you be demolished. He knows where believers will go, but he uses fear to paralyze you from completing your mission.

May we all be like Paul, hard pressed between being with the Lord (which is better) or staying here to further His kingdom (Philippians 1:23-24).

May we all say, *"I have run the race, and I have completed everything God called me to do"* (2 Timothy 4:7-8). That is the believer's hope.

If this is **not** what you believe, or if you do not have the confidence of this, say this prayer with me and **receive Salvation today.**

Let's change your documents which will *change* your destination. For no one gets to the Father except through the Son.

"Jesus answered, 'I am the way and the truth and the life. No one comes to the Father except through me.'" (John 14:6)

Prayer For Salvation

Lord Jesus, I confess that I am a sinner. I believe You are the Son of God and You died on the cross for my sins and rose from the dead. I accept You now as my Lord and Savior. Thank You for forgiving my sins and giving me eternal life. Help me to live for You, walk in Your truth, and fulfill the purpose You've placed on my life. I surrender to Your will. In Jesus' name, Amen.

Woohoo! Heaven rejoices! You have your documents and it was never too late to get them. Just like the criminal's destination changed while on his deathbed next to Jesus Christ on the Cross (Luke 23:43), your destination has **changed.**

And now it's time to grow in your faith. How?

1. Share the good news. You deserve to rejoice.
2. Find a local church or visit one with a family member or friend.
3. Read the Gospels (Personally I'd suggest the Gospel of John first).
4. Meditate on these scriptures for remembrance. It's important to start filling yourself with the Word:
    - John 3:16
    - John 2:2

- Hebrews 10:17
- 2 Corinthians 5:17
- Galatians 2:20
- Ephesians 2:8-9
- Romans 10:9

5. Develop a prayer and reading schedule.
6. You can get a daily devotional
7. Start a Bible Study plan on an app
8. Order the Bible in 365 days book
9. Set time in the morning or night to pray even for 10 minutes
10. Join a Bible Study group for fellowship and accountability
11. Find someone who can disciple you. Most likely this person will be at your new church.

Your new life begins now.

And even if you have accepted Christ, we all must give account. We all will be judged. The way is narrow, **so make decisions with eternity in mind.** The other way is wide and it leads to destruction (Matthew 7:13–14).

Finally, though we are ending this book, I know you and I are still on our own personal journeys of grief. It was not easy. It was quite painful and torturous.

I relapsed.

I gave in.

I backslid.

I forgave.

I wept.

I self-medicated.

I yelled.

I displaced it onto others.

And then eventually… I grieved, lamented, and healed well… *with* God.

After grief comes acceptance.

After acceptance comes purpose.

After purpose comes glory.

After glory comes God.

Because it is in the **glory of the testimony** that the one true and living God is revealed to us.

It only took me growing up out of my agony to understand this because **nothing catches God by surprise.**

He is that wise. He is that good. He is *greater than.*

DEVOTIONAL REFLECTION

READ:

Romans 10:9 — *"If you declare with your mouth, 'Jesus is Lord,' and believe in your heart that God raised Him from the dead, you will be saved."*

REFLECT:

Take some time to reflect on this chapter. Are you confident in your eternal destination? Do you have your documents?

REMEMBER:

"You do not need to fear death as a believer. You do not need to fear the end times or rapture as a believer. This is where the enemy loves to paralyze believers. But trust and know that death or rapture is your passport to heaven.

"Jesus Christ has defeated death, and that is where we should place our hope, our faith, and our destination."

EPILOGUE:
MARY'S LOSS, GOD'S LOVE

Did you know according to the World Health Organization (2025) approximately 1 in 4 pregnancies end in miscarriage, mostly occurring before 28 weeks and 2.6 million babies are stillborn, half of which die in childbirth. Many of these deaths are preventable yet the rising numbers remain heartbreaking.

As someone who works very closely with this population it saddens me to know the impact this has on a mother's emotional, mental, and physical health — sometimes leading to her own life being at risk.

This lends me to think about Mary, Jesus's mother. While she didn't endure a loss prior to or at childbirth, she endured a loss deeper than one can fathom. She watched her Son be crucified as He took on the wrath of God, the sins of this world — disarming every power and principality (Colossians 2:15) and paying the ultimate price. She wasn't just an ordinary mother. She was a mother, who the Holy Spirit came over to conceive (Luke 1:35). I can only imagine the love Jesus had towards His mother. Her task was heavy and holy as she raised a perfect Son, while being an imperfect parent.

In Luke 2:35, Simeon forewarns Mary that a sword will pierce her soul. I am sure she had no idea the depth of this sentiment. We read about her caring for Jesus at the foot of the Cross. She watched Him being bruised, bloodied, beaten, and broken as He gave His life away. The difference between Mary and other mothers is Jesus's life wasn't taken— it was given. This wasn't preventable— it was a prophecy.

Yet, she relates to many mothers who feel the pain from losing their children. The juxtaposition of this all is that the Cross where she grieved, lamented, and mourned is the same Cross where she was met with care, comfort, and compassion. Jesus does not address her as "mother" but as "woman" and tells her to *behold thy son* (John 19:26). This command is two-fold. On one end, Jesus's beloved disciple, John, has now become Mary's son— someone she can depend on and receive care from to fill the voids of her anticipatory grief.

But on the other end, we know this isn't just about Him meeting Mary's needs; He was illustrating that as you behold the Son, at the foot of the Cross, He will fulfill you and take care of you. As Mary was beholding her Son, Jesus Christ, she was seeing Him up close deathly, bloody, and entirely. Just like any mother, she dared not leave His side. And while He was paying the penalty of sin for all mankind, He tenderly provided for her at the same time. Jesus looks beyond Himself and makes provision for Mary.

Like most mothers, I am sure Mary hoped to do something to save Him. But it was not Jesus who needed the saving, it was her— it was the world. And at the foot of the Cross, He gave her hope, a trustworthy person, and a plan in Him. Sometimes as we behold death, as gruesome as it is, we actually can see the beauty in it all… even if it arose three days later.

Mary is the woman Eve could not be, but both of them were necessary. The seed of Eve led to generations that led to the Spirit-filled seed in Mary, which gave birth to Jesus Christ who crushed the serpent's head (Genesis 3:15). In the midst of loss, Mary found love at the Cross.

And how much more God? Did you ever think for a moment that even God, who gave His only begotten Son, also grieved? Doesn't this same God have emotions that surpass our understanding? We see His righteous anger in the Old & New Testament. We see His holy nature. We see His love and mercy on the Cross.

We see Jesus feeling forsaken as He questioned God. We see Him use scripture to fulfil prophecy which served as prayers during His suffering and death. We see His power in the first Church. But did that change, prevent, or redefine who God is? No.

God loved the world so much that He decided to send His only begotten Son as the ultimate sacrifice and offering, making peace with us and God, mediating on our behalf, and being the perfect Lamb of God. There is no more need for bulls or goats blood— the precious blood of Jesus has paid it all (Ephesians 1:7).

It is this love that pleased God to crush Him (Isaiah 53:10) putting Him to grief. It is the Father's love that allowed Jesus to be *"despised and rejected by men, a man of sorrows and acquainted with grief"* (Isaiah 53:3). It is this love that nothing can separate us from, not even death (Romans 8:38).

No one knows grief more than Himself. No one can love more than Himself. He felt what we felt. Thank God we have a High Priest who sympathizes with our weaknesses yet was without sin (Hebrews 4:15). I can't imagine God having to forsake Him — for the beauty of permanent reconciliation sealed by the Spirit of God, by grace through faith.

At the Cross and beyond, we find the Father's love. It was always the greater plan... because God is greater than grief.

RECAP

So, to recap, here are the key things this book has covered:

Remember to include God in your grief. Walking through grief with Him brings transformation, true healing, and a stronger faith along the way. Do not allow grief to distance you from God. Grief is a wilderness, and you need an anchor of hope to hold on to. He is our eternal hope.

Make God bigger than your grief by remembering who He is beyond your pain. Use Scripture to guard your mind when your feelings begin to deceive you, and recall the faithfulness He has shown time after time. You decide how to narrate this journey. He remains on the throne, big enough to surpass your grief and near enough to step into it with you.

Become best friends with the Holy Spirit. Let His presence comfort, strengthen, and empower you to move forward while still accepting what has happened. He is the greatest One to lean on. Fellowship with Him.

Grieve appropriately. Do not honor your late loved ones as if they were gods, but instead remember the good memories and develop healthy ways to keep them alive in your heart. Access practical resources to assist you through this new and sometimes complicated journey. Lament well. Heal well.

Develop a solid community. Choose people you can trust, who remind you of your faith, and who will not allow you to remain in a dark place. You need both accountability and vulnerability. You do not need to do this alone.

Use your time on earth wisely. Be purposeful and remember that death is inevitable. Whether you are here until the rapture or pass away beforehand, your time is limited. Live purposefully now. Build your legacy now. Store up heavenly treasures now.

You have two destinations: Heaven or Hell. Choose eternal life by accepting Jesus Christ as your personal Lord and Savior today. No one comes to the Father except through the Son.

APPENDIX A

Here are the scriptures from the book to help you along the way:

Psalm 10:14 — "But You have seen, for You observe trouble and grief, To repay it by Your hand. The helpless commits himself to You; You are the helper of the fatherless."

Isaiah 58:8 — "Then your light shall break forth like the morning, Your healing shall spring forth speedily, And your righteousness shall go before you; The glory of the Lord shall be your rear guard."

Psalm 30:5 — "Weeping may endure for a night, but joy comes in the morning."

Jeremiah 30:17 — "But I will restore you to health and heal your wounds,' declares the LORD, 'because you are called an outcast, Zion for whom no one cares."

Psalm 22:19 — "But you, Lord, do not be far from me. You are my strength; come quickly to help me."

Psalm 107:20 — *"He sent out his word and healed them; he rescued them from the grave."*

Isaiah 61:3 — *"To all who mourn in Israel, he will give a crown of beauty for ashes, a joyous blessing instead of mourning, festive praise instead of despair. In their righteousness, they will be like great oaks that the LORD has planted for his own glory."*

Isaiah 66:3 — *"As one whom his mother comforts, So I will comfort you; and you shall be comforted in Jerusalem."*

Isaiah 40:31 — *"But those who wait on the Lord will renew their strength. They will mount up with wings like eagles. They will run and not be weary, they will walk and not faint."*

1 Peter 5:7 — *"Cast all your cares on Him because He cares for you."*

Psalm 3:3 — *"You, O Lord, are a shield about me, my glory, and the lifter of my head."*

Revelation 21:4 — *"He will wipe every tear from their eyes. There will be no more death or mourning or crying or pain."*

Job 13:15 — *"Though he slay me, yet will I trust in him..."*

APPENDIX A

Psalm 121:1-2 – *"I will lift up my eyes to the hills – From whence comes my help? My help comes from the Lord, Who made heaven and earth."*

Psalm 3:4 – *"I cried to the LORD with my voice, And He heard me from His holy hill. Selah."*

Psalm 147:3 – *"He heals the brokenhearted and binds up their wounds."*

Romans 12:2 – *"And do not be conformed to this world, but be transformed by the renewing of your mind, that you may prove what is that good and acceptable and perfect will of God."*

Psalm 32:7 – *"You are my hiding place; you will protect me from trouble and surround me with songs of deliverance."*

Nehemiah 8:10 – *"...Do not grieve, for the joy of the Lord is your strength."*

Matthew 11:30 – *"For my yoke is easy, and my burden is light."*

Psalm 34:18 – *"The Lord is near to the brokenhearted and saves those who are crushed in spirit."*

Deuteronomy 31:8 – *"It is the Lord who goes before you. He will be with you; He will not leave you or forsake you. Do not fear or be dismayed."*

Lamentations 3:22-23 – *"Because of the Lord's great love we are not consumed, for his compassions never fail. They are new every morning; great is your faithfulness."*

Psalm 119:114 – *"You are my hiding place and my shield; I put my hope in Your Word."*

Psalm 119:130 – *"The unfolding of your words gives light; it gives understanding to the simple."*

Exodus 15:26 – *"I am the LORD, who heals you."*

Matthew 9:21 – *"If I only touch His cloak, I will be healed."*

Psalm 30:11 – *"You turned my wailing into dancing; you removed my sackcloth and clothed me with joy."*

Psalm 40:3 – *"He has given me a new song to sing, a hymn of praise to our God. Many will see what he has done and be amazed. They will put their trust in the LORD."*

ABOUT THE AUTHOR

Lisa Ann-Marie Stanford is a writer from Maryland who's passionate about guiding young women, sharing her faith in Jesus, and encouraging others to seek God's Kingdom first. Having walked through deep personal loss, she writes honestly and from the heart, using her own story to point to God's faithful restoration. Lisa also owns and operates her own mental health care practice, where she continues her mission of supporting others through compassionate care. This book highlights those losses and the healing that followed, offering hope to others carrying the weight of grief. When she's not writing, Lisa enjoys time with family and friends, serving in ministry, at her local church—Harvest Intercontinental Church Olney, reading a good book, and going on solo dates.

ACKNOWLEDGEMENTS

Writing a book is both challenging and rewarding. I am grateful for my village and those who continue to push me to fulfill the God-breathed purposes attached to my life.

I am thankful for my family.

I want to especially honor my mother. You have instilled in me strength, faith, and rich spiritual seeds. Without your prayers, I don't know where I would be today. I'm deeply grateful that we both stand healed from the losses we've faced. It's incredible to witness how what God began in you is now flourishing in me. I honor you, and I rise up and call you blessed (Proverbs 31:28).

Additionally, I want to thank my sister, Tracy. Since childhood, you've been a constant source of protection, love, and support. Thank you for your years of sacrifice and selflessness. I'm so grateful to have you in my corner and deeply thankful for the restoration between us. It makes my heart smile to see you win, grow, and succeed- and that'll never change. I love you dearly.

I also want to acknowledge my siblings—Sharon, Christopher, Mark, Michelle, and Roy Jr. You are a part of me, just as I am a part of you. I'm grateful for the bond we share and the healing we've experienced. I know Daddy would be so proud. I only wish he could see us now. The Stanford name lives on.

I'm also deeply appreciative of my cousins—Aisha, Deserea, Destiny, Devon, Darnell—and my Aunt Joan. The memories we've shared as a family are forever etched in my heart. I love you all so very much. A special thank-you as well to my extended family, both near and far, for your continued love and support. Truly, God has restored more than what I lost—more than what we lost.

A big shoutout to my church family. I have grown in the things of the Lord because of the rich teaching, discipleship, and love this community has poured into me. My pastors—from my youth through adulthood—have played a vital role in shaping who I am today. Thank you for reminding me of my identity in Christ when I lost sight of it, and for the countless ways you've invested in me. Bishop Johnson and Lady Chrys Johnson, thank you for your exemplary leadership and grace. Thank you to everyone who prayed for my father during his battle with cancer. A special thank-you to Elder Nestor for praying with him every single day until his final breath. Your faithfulness and compassion will never be forgotten.

I am grateful for my mentors. Grief is messy, and each of you has walked with me through its many phases. Some of you have known me since my youth; others entered my life as I tried to piece things back together as an adult, and some of you returned to help me push out destiny in this season. No matter the season, thank you all for holding my hand when life felt unbearable. When others judged me, you chose to sit with me (literally) in the mess — unbothered by the stench. Thank you for reminding me that there's a rainbow at the end of the storm and for covering me with love, free of judgment or shame.

I am grateful for my friends.

Many of you were present when this all occurred. You've witnessed the growing pains and sometimes felt the backend of it too. Your unwavering shoulder to lean on, support, celebration, tears and prayers have been a shield of encouragement. Even when I wanted to give up, you all have always pushed me to keep going one way or another. I love you all. As the Word says, indeed, a good friendship refreshes the soul. A special shoutout to my best friend, Christine, who stood by my side through both losses. You were there in my dad's final hour, and you held my baby boy after he passed. You are a steadfast friend, and I'm forever grateful.

Lastly, I want to extend my heartfelt thanks to my publisher, Great Books.

Roy, I'm especially grateful for the way you approached this project — not as just another job or publication, but with genuine care, relatability, discernment, and patience. Your constant encouragement made this more than a professional collaboration; it became ministry. This book would not have come to life without you. I can't wait to create the next one. I highly recommend this publishing company!